SHARING
RESPONSIBILITY

—

SHARING
RESPONSIBILITY

—

LARRY MAY

The University of Chicago Press
Chicago and London

Larry May is professor of philosophy at Washington University in St. Louis.

The University of Chicago Press, Chicago 60637
The University of Chicago Press, Ltd., London
© 1992 by The University of Chicago
All rights reserved. Published 1992
Printed in the United States of America
01 00 99 98 97 96 95 94 93 92   5 4 3 2 1

ISBN (cloth): 0-226-51168-5

Library of Congress Cataloging-in-Publication Data

May, Larry.
    Sharing responsibility / Larry May.
        p.   cm.
    Includes bibliographical references and index.
    ISBN 0-226-51168-5 (alk. paper)
    1. Responsibility.   2. Social ethics.   3. Social groups—Moral and
ethical aspects.   4. Existential ethics.   I. Title.
    BJ1451.M36   1992
    170—dc20   92-12658
                                                                    CIP

For Marilyn

Contents

Contents

—

Acknowledgments

This book was stimulated by a discussion I had with Normand Laurendeau, who consulted me about a yearly seminar on ethics he teaches to seniors in mechanical engineering. I couldn't think of a book that set out a theory of moral responsibility that was applicable to the large number of cases concerning membership in groups; so I began writing such a book. I am grateful to Norm, and also to Bill McBride who was very encouraging, especially as I became increasingly convinced that the literature in continental social philosophy could provide a rich resource for a new understanding of shared moral responsibility.

Many people read various versions of the chapters contained in this volume. Their discussion of my ideas has made them come alive. Here is a list of those whose comments most stuck in my memory: Roger Gardner, Patricia Greenspan, Russell Hardin, John Deigh, Christine Korsgaard, Peter French, David Copp, John Ladd, Howard McGary, Adrian Piper, Laurence Thomas, Marcia Baron, Dorothy Leland, Lilly Russow, Patricia Curd, William Rowe, Paul Eisenberg, Jerry Kohn, Gertrude Ezorski, Suzanne Jacobitti, Virginia Held, and Leslie Frances. I am especially grateful to the following individuals who read and commented on earlier versions of the entire manuscript: Hugh LaFollette, Iris Young, Robert Louden, Norm Laurendeau, Rod Bertolet, and Marilyn Friedman. In addition, I owe a large debt of gratitude to Marilyn Friedman and Bill McBride, who discussed my ideas over the course of many meals together.

Earlier versions of three chapters appeared as articles in the following journals: chapter 3, as "Insensitivity and Moral Responsibility," in *The Journal of Value Inquiry* 26, no. 1 (January 1992), pp. 7–22; chapter 6, as "Collective Inaction and Shared Responsibility," in *Nous* 24 (1990), pp. 269–77; and chapter 7, "Philosophers and Political Responsibility," in *Social Research* 56 (Winter 1989). In addition, chapter 8 appeared in my co-edited anthology, *Collective Responsibil-*

ity, published by Rowman and Littlefield 1991. I am grateful for permission to reprint these essays. Several chapters were read first at conferences held at Brown University, the University of Chicago, the University of Utah, and Indiana University, as well as several meetings of the American Philosophical Association. I am grateful for those who took part in these discussions.

David Brent has been very encouraging throughout this process. I thank him and the rest of the University of Chicago Press staff, especially Deborah Koomjian. Also I would like to thank Debi Katz and Dorothy Fleck for clerical assistance in the final stages of this project.

What counts is that a wrong has been committed. . . .
As citizens we must prevent wrong-doing since the
world we all share, wrong-doer, wrong-sufferer and
spectator, is at stake.
  Hannah Arendt, "Thinking and Moral Considerations"
—

This taking upon ourselves the consequences for things
we are entirely innocent of, is the price we pay for the
fact that we live our lives not by ourselves
but . . . [within] a human community.
    Hannah Arendt, "Collective Responsibility"

Introduction

The central claim of this book is that people should see themselves as sharing responsibility for various harms perpetrated by, or occurring within, their communities. The book is divided into three main parts, each corresponding to an area of expansion of the domain of responsibility that is warranted once one accepts the notion of shared responsibility. In the first part, I argue for responsibility based on one's attitudes, especially those attitudes that make harm within a community more likely to occur. In the second part, I argue for responsibility based on failures to act, both individual omissions and collective inaction, especially as those failures increase the likelihood and scope of harm that one's community perpetrates. And in the third part, I argue for increased responsibility based on the various roles and positions people assume within their communities.

Specifically, I argue that the members of communities should come to see themselves as personally sharing in responsibility for the harms of their communities, even when these members did not participate directly in the harm and even, in some cases, when these members could not have prevented the harm. The notion of shared responsibility underlies this claim and involves an enriching as well as an expanding of the domain of moral and political responsibility. Seeing ourselves as sharing in responsibility for what our communities do will cause us to look as closely at our roles, attitudes, and omissions as we currently look at our explicit behavior. Seeing responsibility as shared also causes an expansion of our vocabulary to account for the various gradations of fault of the disparate members of a community. In this sense, shame, regret, and taint are as important as guilt.

Throughout this book I provide a view of moral responsibility that is greatly inspired by German and French philosophers who wrote in the immediate aftermath of the Nazi reign of terror. Philosophers such as Jean-Paul Sartre, Karl Jaspers, and Hannah Arendt tried to

1

explain why their fellow citizens failed to act to prevent the horrors they witnessed. All three of these philosophers turned to the theory of existentialism to explain the human failures they experienced, as well as to ground an alternative view of moral responsibility. Specifically, all three thinkers described how the world might be different if people adopted a concept of shared responsibility. It is my intent to modify this view, which I will call social existentialism, to make it more accessible and more plausible to those of us at the end of the twentieth century who are again reconsidering our moral responsibilities in light of such situations as apartheid and world hunger.

While there are many arguments presented in this book, the main thrust of my writing, like that of the existentialists of the earlier part of the twentieth century, is to provide a vision of our place in the world. The overall vision is presented as itself deserving of serious consideration, regardless of whether or not the arguments supporting the various pieces of the vision are themselves each plausible to a particular reader. This approach is a return to earlier ways of doing philosophy, when merit was awarded to views that were either in general immediately appealing to many people, or so provocative that many people came to reconsider some of their most deeply held beliefs. As with any systematic presentation, even concerning only a part of morality, it is not possible to provide rigorous arguments in support of every aspect of the view or against all reasonable counterarguments. This book will succeed, though, if its moral theses, often dismissed as implausible by contemporary theorists, are placed in a context that makes them harder to dismiss.

1. Social Existentialism

Existentialism is no longer in fashion. The excitement reserved for philosophical views that capture the popular imagination is now extended to such movements as hermeneutics, deconstruction, and other forms of postmodernism. These movements have all, in various ways, eschewed politics and social criticism. And Mary Midgley has made a similar point about some of analytic philosophy in her essay "The Flight from Blame."[1] With all of its faults, existentialism had the great benefit of inspiring people to see themselves as responsible for the social and political ills of their times. It stressed responsibility to such an extent that only the most politically engaged individual could be sure of meeting the existentialist challenge.

Ours is still an age that is critical of authority, and if responsibility is going to make a comeback it will probably have to be without the authority of a god or a charismatic leader. In this one sense, then, existentialism still should speak to all of us. For existentialism was born out of the ashes of "the death of god" at the end of the nineteenth century, a death that involved suspending faith in all nonhuman solutions as well as turning away from all easy answers. This is not to say that the often problematic metaphysics of existentialism should be revived, but rather that a social philosophy steeped in everyday existence instead of in some kind of transcendent authority is still worth attention, especially if it offers a constructive alternative to the nihilism of deconstruction and the quietism of a great deal of analytic philosophy.

There are really two different views which have been called existentialist. One view, which derives historically from certain interpretations of the early Sartre and Camus, sees the self as a centerless fabrication of the individual will. Each person is radically free to construct himself or herself into whatever person he or she chooses. There is no essence of each person, but only each person's chosen existence. Another view, which derives from Heidegger, Jaspers, and the later Sartre, sees the self as a social construct, as a function of the interplay of history, social conditioning, and the chosen behavior of the individual person. Of course, in this view, the being that does the choosing is itself a product of society. But it is possible for a single person to choose which societal influences he or she will be exposed to, and hence which kind of self he or she will become (at least within certain limits). Here, also, there is no essence of the self; it is social experience or existence, as well as individual choosing, that constructs the self. It is this latter, social, existentialism, that I find worth reviving and advocating.

Both forms of existentialism stress that attitudes as well as explicit behavior must be scrutinized to see if the individual is living up to his or her responsibilities. Even when there is seemingly nothing that one can *do* to prevent an evil in the world, one has a responsibility to distance oneself from that evil, at the very least by not condoning it. Being morally or politically responsible is something that takes a lot of work; it is not merely a matter of conforming to a list of minimal rules. Existentialist responsibility is a heavy burden on all of us, one from which the members of a highly self-indulgent age would flee.

Continental philosophers who have been critical of existentialism are not the only, or even the central, target of a revived existentialist project, for there are many aspects of contemporary analytic moral theory that urge us to narrow rather than expand our domain of responsibility. The British philosophers Bernard Williams and Stuart Hampshire, as well as a number of younger American philosophers, most notably Susan Wolf, have urged that it is a mistake to set the requirements of morality too high.[2] If Gauguin had been more responsible, he would not have forsaken his wife and children for the pleasures of Tahiti, and he would not have produced great works of art. Saintly or morally heroic conduct is often not appropriate, so these thinkers have argued, especially when living the fully responsible life gets in the way of the pursuit of aesthetic, intellectual, or even comfort-oriented values.

To be sure, there have been reactions to the retreat from responsibility. Virtue theorists and communitarians have recently risen to the challenge; but many have espoused a politically conservative (indeed often reactionary) political agenda. There are very few cries of "Back to Aristotle" that are not conjoined with cries of "Back to St. Benedict" (or Thomas Aquinas or John Calvin). Communitarian ethical perspectives emphasize a respect for tradition, for the values that have characterized a particular community. But often those values are at odds with the liberation of groups that have "traditionally" been the subject of adverse treatment by a community. And yet a moral and political philosophy ought to promote, surely not repress, such liberationist projects. For example, apartheid in South Africa is supported by a religiously inspired tradition that, so it is often claimed, cannot be dismantled without destruction of that community. It may be, though, that the community traditions supporting apartheid are simply not worth saving, and that the traditional values of that community do not have any special weight merely because they do in fact undergird a stable community.

From a social existentialist perspective, community membership creates new possibilities and also new responsibilities for individuals. Existentialism, especially that espoused by Karl Jaspers, recognized this better than any other twentieth-century theory.[3] Such a recognition is based on a serious appraisal of the actual events of our century. Like Jaspers, I will locate my theorizing in concrete experience, especially the experience of those who have been the victims of community oppression. Insofar as communities enable individuals to do more harm than they could otherwise do, communities also create more responsibility for those whose lives are woven into the fabric of the community itself.

2. Shared Attitudes

The central thesis of the first part of this book is that it is appropriate to attribute responsibility to people for some of their attitudes. I argue for the controversial claim that people who share certain attitudes, such as racist attitudes, share responsibility for harms that result from their attitudes, even if the individuals in question do not directly cause the harms themselves. In the chapters of this section I draw heavily on the writings of Jean-Paul Sartre.

Western moral philosophy in the last two hundred years has generally restricted the realm of moral appraisal to the intentions and actions that are the result of a person's conscious deliberation and will. Against this tradition I will argue that aspects of the self, in particular certain attitudes, should be considered the responsibility of the self, even when those aspects are not fully under the control of the person's will. Two main theses undergird my analysis. First, I argue for an expanded understanding of the ways that a person can influence herself or himself. I develop an existential conception of consciousness, which stresses that some attitudes are the products of quasi-conscious deliberation over which a person is at least partially in control, and for which responsibility, at least to some degree, can be attributed to the person. Second, I develop a virtue-theoretic understanding of character, which stresses that certain attitudes are strongly influenced by a person's sensitivity to, or ignorance of, the way that attitudes cause harm to others. Under certain conditions, responsibility should be shared by people who share character-based attitudes.

In contemporary moral philosophy, both of the dominant theoretical traditions, deontological ethics and utilitarian ethics, are concerned with the assessment of actions that have been produced by a rational, intentional act of will. Since a person's attitudes are not normally chosen after rational deliberation, it is thought that attitudes lie outside the proper domain of moral assessment. Both types of ethical theory follow Immanuel Kant in viewing attitudes as too greatly influenced by instinct and inclination for the individual person to be able to exercise the kind of control that constitutes moral agency.[4]

Many people are not aware of the origin of their attitudes, and hence regard their attitudes as immune to change through deliberation of any sort. One of the functions of such strategies as psychoanalysis, psychotherapy, and consciousness raising, as well as various self-reflective processes, is to help people identify their attitudes and learn how to change them. The reason that some attitudes can be reflected upon and changed is that these attitudes are partially cognitive, in that they reside at the quasi-conscious level of awareness. I will develop an existential understanding of how attitudes are formed and changed. In doing so, I will defend the claim that there is a type of awareness, pre-reflective awareness, that is not fully conscious but is still under the control of the person.

Virtue theory stresses the importance of disposition and emotion in the formation of a person's character. Virtue theorists have argued that too much emphasis has been placed on the will, and on a restricted conception of self-control, in theories of morality.[5] In this vein, I will contend that even if attitudes are not *fully* under the control of the will, they should still be subject to moral appraisal, so long as they are at least *partially* under the control of the will. This thesis is defended in detail in chapter 1. An existentialist theory of responsibility is based on choice but is only partially cognitivist. Such a theory allows a large space for semi-conscious and pre-reflective choice. As I will argue, an expanded account of choice allows for such notions as negligence in a way that standard choice-oriented models of responsibility do not. Rather than focusing exclusively on current choices, an existentialist theory of responsibility considers the way that past choices have created a context for the capacity to control the present. In this sense, an existentialist theory of responsibility mixes elements of choice and control.

Sharing responsibility for attitudes does not require that we only ascribe responsibility for those attitudes that are *fully* under the control of a person's will. Instead, I advocate a weaker requirement, namely, that a person is responsible for those attitudes that he or she could partially change (or could have partially changed) *and* that it is reasonable to say the person should change (or should have changed). In this view, a person may be negligently ignorant of his or her attitudes and hence responsible for these attitudes, even though the person is not fully aware of having the attitudes or of how fully to change the attitudes. I will place attitudes into the class of things one can be reasonably expected to change when it is understood that they are likely to be productive of harm. I examine the case of racist attitudes, contending that those who have racist attitudes in a community in which racial violence has occurred share responsibility for these harms. The argument for this claim will be advanced in chapter 2.

Annette Baier proposes that changes of mind concerning conventionally held beliefs are like "indigestible late fruit, sour even when ripe."[6] Part of the difficulty in changing conventional attitudes is that most of us spend a great deal of our lives selectively ignoring many things that, should we bring them to self-consciousness, would still prove difficult to change. Attitudes, especially such deep-seated ones as are involved in stereotypes, may prove difficult to change, but the difficulty is normally something that can be at least partially overcome, as sociological studies have shown. It is important for people to view their attitudes with constant vigilance and self-criticism. Sensitive members of a community will subject not only their actions but also their attitudes to such self-criticism in order to meet the most basic moral responsibility: to be a fully moral person. This thesis is further examined in chapter 3.

3. Omissions and Responsibility in Groups

In the second part of this book I will discuss how individuals, when they are in large groups or institutions, often find themselves failing to prevent harms they would have prevented on their own. And yet the harm that could be prevented, individually or collectively, within groups is often more serious than harm caused by isolated individuals. Once again we confront the problem that individuals often do not take responsibility for what their groups have done or could have done, because they do not recognize that they share responsibility for what their groups do. In chapter 4, I explore the various ways that groups transform the attitudes and values of their members, often reducing the sense of shared responsibility.

In the early 1960s, Hannah Arendt was asked by the *New Yorker* to cover the trial of Adolph Eichmann. After several months of watching the trial and studying Eichmann's past, she came to a startling conclusion about this person who had been personally responsible for sending thousands of Jews to their deaths in Hitler's concentration camps. Eichmann was really not significantly different from most of the people she knew. If he was different at all, it was only in that he displayed an almost uncanny ability not to think about what he was doing. This habit had developed over many years and was brought about, she hypothesized, by his belief that in order to provide well for his family he had to be both dutiful and clever in carrying out the orders he was given. But in order to be able to sleep at night, he couldn't both do an excellent job at work and also think self-reflectively about what he was doing. Arendt coined the phrase "the banality of evil" to characterize the normal, nonugly face of those who, in groups, are capable of doing acts of great harm, or of failing to prevent fellow community members from engaging in such harm. The normal tendency toward thoughtlessness seems to get worse when people are in groups or organizations.[7]

The first way in which individual behavior changes in groups concerns the way that institutional groups break up problems into constituent elements so that no one person feels responsible for the whole problem. Not only are strong reasons provided to think of oneself only in compartmentalized ways, but the institutions to which one belongs seem to have taken Adam Smith's old notion of the "division of labor" to great extremes. By chopping projects into so many smaller units, responsibility is diffused. One antidote to this tendency is to expand the notion of moral negligence so that it encompasses the neglect to ascertain what the likely consequences are of the joint actions to which one contributes. An expanded notion of negligence, especially in professional life, can aid significantly in encouraging people to look to the consequences of the projects to which they are asked to contribute. In chapter 5, I will argue for an expanded notion of moral negligence.

Groups affect individual behavior in a second morally relevant way. In the famous case of Kitty Genovese, thirty-eight residents of an apartment building failed to do anything, even failed to call the police, over a half-hour period during which Genovese, a fellow resident, was beaten, stabbed repeatedly, and eventually killed by an assailant on the street outside the apartment building. Each person thought that someone else in the building either would call or surely already had called the police; after all, only a phone call was required. Responsibility is diffused in such a group, especially when action is not required from all or even a large segment of the group. People think, if they think at all, "Let the other person do it—I have too much to lose."[8] I examine this problem of collective inaction in chapter 6.

Individual conscience and standards of professional negligence normally operate rather well to curtail unethical conduct in the face-to-face dealings of individuals. But, as I have been arguing, both individual conscience and professional responsibility are hindered in important ways by the functioning of large-scale organizations like universities or corporations, or of smaller-scale groups like Kitty Genovese's apartment community. Why are people so reluctant, when they are in groups, to act to prevent harm? I argue that one important answer is that people often do not conceive of themselves as sharing responsibility with their fellow group members for harms which they could have prevented by acting alone or in concert with others. I draw on the insights of Hannah Arendt to argue in favor of a revival of this concept in contemporary life, especially as a way of understanding responsibility for omissions and inaction of groups and within groups where harm occurs.

4. Communities and Shared Values

In the third part of this book, I explore the notion of community membership as a locus of responsibility. Again, I take as my point of departure writings by existentialists such as Karl Jaspers. In the concluding chapter I attempt to connect my views with debates concerning communitarianism. These chapters are deeply rooted in the experience I know best: chapter 7 concerns the responsibilities arising from being a member of a professional academic group, and chapter 8 explores responsibility in a university community. But an attempt is made to generalize to all forms of community membership. Specifically, I argue that the benefits of community membership accrue only at the cost of increased responsibility for the members of communities.

In a previous book, *The Morality of Groups*,[9] I argued that contemporary ethical theory needs to be more concerned with the way that moral judgments and intuitions change when a group rather than an individual person is the object of moral scrutiny. Given the prevalence of organized and unorganized social groups in contemporary society, justice and responsibility generally cannot be understood by looking only to the individual, isolated from his or her social environment. Rather, social groups such as corporations, teams, mobs, associations, ethnic groups, or residents of a public housing complex, can affect our judgments about justice and responsibility. In the earlier work, I centered my attention on the attribution of moral categories *to* groups. In *Sharing Responsibility*, I turn my attention to the way that individuals *within* groups should conceive of their moral and political responsibilities. I urge that we direct our attention toward group membership as an important source of heightened personal responsibility.

In these final chapters I indicate why communities are important loci of moral value, by considering and expanding arguments from political philosophy, moral theory, and applied ethics. I argue that what existentialists, communitarians, and virtue theorists hold in common is a discontent with the too-narrow focus of deontological and utilitarian moral theory. I share this discontent. I argue in chapter 7 that philosophers as well as other writers and teachers should conceive of their political and moral responsibilities much more broadly than they generally do. They should take responsibility for the foreseeable consequences of their writings and teachings, as well as for the harmful conduct of their fellow professional-group members.

The moral landscape for most people contains rigid notions of individual obligation and guilt. But there is much more to that moral landscape. When moral theorists arbitrarily restrict the domain of morality to part of this landscape, they risk misconceiving the point of morality for most people. In particular, group shame and moral taint need to be recognized as additional components of this landscape, since they play integral roles in the moral experiences that most people have. Chapter 8 deals with how these components of morality both stress the way that people are interconnected in groups and pay attention to the communal interests and responsibilities that individuals have because of their group memberships.

In contemporary communitarian theory, one school of thought (epitomized in the writings of Alasdair MacIntyre) has stressed the close relationship between being virtuous and conforming one's behavior to a social role. Seemingly, if one were to conform one's behavior to social roles with single-mindedness, one would be conscientious and one would be more virtuous than someone who conformed to social roles only half-heartedly or not at all. At the extreme would be the person who always scrupulously pursued the social roles he or she was placed in. But such a person would lack the resources critically to evaluate the roles, and would not be able to aid in the progressive development of the community away from traditions that unfairly discriminated against certain subgroups within that community. In some cases, it is more virtuous to reject or reshape one's social roles rather than conscientiously to conform to those roles.

I argue that we need an expanded notion of responsibility which includes responsibility for some harms our communities have committed, with or without our participation. I develop the notion of shared agency to capture the idea that people are empowered by, and also aid in the empowerment of, their fellow community members. In this sense, all of the members of a community share in what each member does, and each member should feel some responsibility for what the other members do. When people are harmed by community practices, even those community members who did not participate in those practices should at least feel tainted by them. Here sharing responsibility and taking responsibility for one's community merge. Such a merger is presented, in the final chapter, as a "liberationist communitarian" view which contrasts with the conservatism of most community-oriented moral and political theories.

PART ONE

Attitudes, Agency, and Responsibility

—

ONE

Existentialism, Self, and Voluntariness

This chapter concerns the interrelations among three concepts: the self, voluntariness, and moral responsibility. Normally, one's conception of the self will affect the way in which one conceives the range of things for which a person may be morally responsible. In the first section, I develop a preliminary view of the concept of moral responsibility, explaining how we should expand the normal domain of responsibility. In the second section, I present an existentialist theory of the self and relate this theory to the difficult case of responsibility for one's mental states. In the third section I present a sample of nonexistentialist views which share certain features with my own view. In the fourth section, I critically assess a very recent attempt to suggest that responsibility for one's mental states must lead us to disconnect responsibility from voluntariness.

1. Responsibility and Agency

Let us begin with a typical model of moral responsibility for a harm:

A person is morally responsible for a given harm or character defect if:

(a) the person's conduct played a significant causal role in that harm or defect; and

(b) the person's conduct was blameworthy or it was morally faulty in some other way.

Joel Feinberg points out that there should be a third factor, which he calls the causal relevance factor, positing a connection between (a) and (b).[1] So let us add:

(c) the aspect of the act that was faulty was also one of the aspects in virtue of which it was a cause of the harm.

Normally when someone is responsible for a harm, that person is blamed for that harm. Blameworthiness is often conceived on the model of legal liability, having to do with voluntariness and intentionality as well as the violation of some norm. But, as I will argue later, there are morally faulty types of behavior other than those warranting blame, including behavior that warrants shame, remorse, regret, and feelings of taint. These types of moral fault are not best understood on the model of legal guilt.

There is a tight relationship between causal agency ("a" above) and responsibility. But moral responsibility is not the same as causal responsibility, for people are not responsible for all of the things they cause. With a few important exceptions, people are generally morally responsible only for those things they *voluntarily* cause. And in addition, as Feinberg's third factor makes clear, people are only responsible for some harm or defect if there is a connection between the act that caused the harm or defect and the faultiness of that act.

In my view, there are things for which a person can be morally responsible other than those harms or benefits that one directly causes. Defects, especially in states of mind or character, that make it more likely that someone will cause harm are also things for which a person can be responsible. In subsequent chapters I will argue in detail for the claim that people are responsible for various attitudes (including insensitivity and racism) and not just for the effects of their explicit behavior. Here, it seems to me, states of mind are themselves often effects of what a person voluntarily chooses to do, although these are effects on a person's own self rather than effects on other selves. In cases of both external and internal effects, what a person has voluntarily chosen is the key for my analysis.

The view of responsibility I will defend in what follows is existentialist in inspiration because of the emphasis placed on what people voluntarily choose. Existentialists, especially Sartre, Camus, and Jaspers, greatly expanded the domain of the voluntary, as we will see in the next section of this chapter. But they remained committed to the idea that people should only be held, or hold themselves, responsible for what they could, at least partially, control. The emphasis on self-control is not, though, as individualistic in orientation as one might suppose. For *social* existentialism, to which I subscribe, stresses the way that our choices are greatly affected by the groups of which we are members. Self-control is to be understood as partial control over the self by the self's use of social factors that shape who the self is. I will say much more about this later. But I want to stress that responsibility should remain connected to what people decide to do with their lives, and not become merely a kind of moral strict liability.

In all types of responsibility, there is the root idea that people should have to "respond" in some appropriate way (to their fellow community members, to their god, to themselves, etc.) when something they have chosen to do is faulty, in the sense that it violates a moral norm.[2] Insofar as people act in ways that are voluntary, they should have to stand ready, even if only in the court of conscience, to give an account of why their acts are justifiable. And the basis of this intuitive idea is that people are not merely isolated beings, but that they are members of groups in which it matters to other members what they choose to do. Like justice, responsibility begins with voluntary choices. But unlike justice, responsibility will apply even when the voluntary choices seem only to affect the states of mind or character traits of the self alone.

Responsibility stems from agency, and yet agency itself begins in the deep recesses of the self. The kind of behavior we engage in does not arise overnight but is normally a function of many successive layers of choosing over the course of a life. For this reason, responsibility is not confined to those isolated actions which have effects on others, but also includes those decisions that form the self into the kind of agent it is and that influence the way that self then acts in the world. Since the self plays such a large role in the determination of behavior, it seems quite reasonable to include its effects on internal states as an integral part of that larger compass of responsibility normally thought to be restricted only to the self's effects on external behavior. If some variation of behaviorism turns out to be true, then who the self is just is the way the self behaves. But this does not mean that there are not internal as well as external effects of this behavior. One can be responsible for both of these effects. This is at least the way in which I will understand moral responsibility.

In general, I understand responsibility to be based on the self's responses concerning its choices; hence responsibility is intimately connected with self-control. Self-control involves some type of freedom of the self allowing for a choice that is not forced upon the agent by factors outside the self's conscious understanding of itself. But as many authors have recently argued, the kind of freedom required for self-control cannot be the freedom to do otherwise, since so much of what we are capable of doing is determined by genetic and environmental factors. Harry Frankfurt provides a good example here:

> Jones decides for reasons of his own to do something, then someone threatens him with a very sharp penalty (so harsh that any reasonable person would submit to the threat) unless he does precisely that, and Jones does it. . . . The threat impressed him, as it would any reasonable man, and he would have submitted to it wholeheartedly if he had not already made a decision that coincided with the one demanded of him.[3]

Here we find that an environmental factor, the threat, eliminates the possibility that Jones could act otherwise than the way he in fact acted. But the reason that he acted had to do with his own decision. In this case, Jones seems to display self-control sufficient for moral agency, even though he does not possess the ability to act otherwise. What he does possess, though, is the ability to make decisions that have effects on his behavior, or that constitute his behavior.

The kind of choice that must be available to the agent for the agent to have self-control is the freedom to reach decisions about his or her future conduct *and* the freedom to initiate action that may bring those decisions to fruition. In the case mentioned above, Jones must be able to reach decisions and Jones himself must be able to play some role in the accomplishment of various ends he decides to pursue. These two components of self-control correspond to the agency component (a) in the analysis I provided above. From what I have already said, it should be evident that the second part of agency is not the same as the ability to do otherwise. All that is required is potential efficaciousness but not the full-blown freedom involved in the ability to *do* otherwise. The agency component of moral responsibility concerns the ability for the self to be able to make decisions on its own, and for its inner life potentially to have an impact on external behavior. In the second section of this chapter I will defend an existentialist account of the self, which has the two components I sketched above. And in the third section, I will briefly survey some views in the history of philosophy that are similar to my own.

2. Existentialism and the Self

Existentialism has provided a rich literature on the subject of responsibility. Early existentialists stressed personal responsibility, while later existentialists were more concerned with social and political responsibilities. While I will draw extensively from both types of existentialism, I am most sympathetic with the social existentialists who concerned themselves with the way groups of people come to share responsibility for the world's harms. A *personal* existentialist account of responsibility stresses that there are many aspects of life over which one has at least some control, even though one may be unaware of this fact. One is responsible for all of those things over which one has control, and responsibility for one's states of mind is added to the normal range of things for which responsibility is properly assigned.

A *social* existentialist account of responsibility extends this point beyond the self to the larger domain of things over which a person could exert influence. Here there are many things that a person may not have directly caused, that nonetheless it was under his or her power to influence. Regardless of whether a person is aware of these things, if they are things over which that person could exert influence, they may be things for which a person is at least partially responsible. I describe my project as a social existentialist project because I adopt this expanded domain of responsibility, arguing that most of one's responsibilities are shared rather than uniquely one's own. In addition, I incorporate various personal existentialist notions into my analysis, such as responsibility for attitudes and other states of mind, but I focus on the way those attitudes facilitate social harm or benefit.

According to the most extreme personal existentialist view of the self, each of us is radically free to be the person he or she chooses to be at any given time. The self is largely characterless, insofar as character is meant to stand for that fixed core, or essence, of the self. Most people may choose to be relatively the same selves from week to week, but that is their choice. They could have chosen otherwise, for there is no determinate structure of the self over time. While there may be actions that the self is seemingly determined to do, there is always the possibility of choosing how one regards one's behavior. And even in the most determined circumstances, there are always at least two alternative courses of action open to the agent, namely, to do what one is doing or to end one's life.

In *The Myth of Sisyphus*, Albert Camus reinterprets a Greek myth to illustrate his conception of the self as radically free and responsible.

> The gods had condemned Sisyphus to ceaselessly rolling a rock to the top of a mountain, whence the stone would fall back of its own weight. They had thought with some reason that there is no more dreadful punishment than

futile and hopeless labor. . . . As for the myth, one sees merely the whole effort of a body straining to raise the huge stone, to roll it and push it up a slope a hundred times over; one sees the face screwed up, the cheek tight against the stone, the shoulder bracing the clay covered mass, the foot wedging it, the fresh start with arms outstretched, the wholly human security of two earth-clotted hands. At the very end of this long effort measured by skyless space and time without depth, the purpose is achieved. Then Sisyphus watches the stone rush down in a few moments toward that lower world whence he will have to push it up again toward the summit. He goes back down to the plain.[4]

Yet Camus contends that Sisyphus is not defeated by even so deterministic a punishment. For each time that Sisyphus consciously chooses to go back down the mountain without showing any signs of despair, he defeats the gods. "There is no fate that cannot be surmounted by scorn," Camus tells us. And later he adds, "Sisyphus teaches the higher fidelity that negates the gods and raises rocks. . . . The struggle itself toward the heights is enough to fill a man's heart. One must imagine Sisyphus happy."[5]

This interpretation of the myth is meant to symbolize the struggle that each person experiences, even when it is realized that life is absurd in its pointlessness. According to Camus, one can either accept or reject one's fate, and in so doing one shows oneself to be "the master of his days." Radical freedom of the self does not necessarily mean that one is in control of every aspect of one's life. Rather radical freedom of the self involves the ability to shape most, if not all, of one's responses to the world, to be the master of one's inner self. For such a view, the self must be mainly identified with its beliefs, and this is indeed the position that Camus takes:

> The principle can be established that for a man who does not cheat, what he believes to be true must determine his action. Belief in the absurdity of existence must then dictate his conduct. It is legitimate to wonder, clearly and without false pathos, whether a conclusion of this importance requires forsaking as rapidly as possible an incomprehensible condition. I am speaking, of course, of men inclined to be in harmony with themselves.[6]

Camus's general point is that one's fate is never sealed until the self has given up believing that change is possible. And, I take it, even this act of giving up is itself a choice that can be revoked at some later time, if one has not also opted out of one's absurd life altogether.

I do not support such an extreme version of existentialism, but I am drawn to many of Camus's evocative images. Camus's conception of responsibility is overly individualistic and misses the importance of groups in the picture he paints. It is true that we are all partially responsible for many of the defects of our selves or the harms of the world. But because our lives are interdependent with the lives of others it is misleading to speak of people as being radically free. We are not free to change the world overnight, although in combination with others we often are able to change the world over the long run. Because of our dependence on the help of others to change the world, it makes more sense to speak of shared rather than personal responsibility in a great many cases over which we could exert some control. The option of suicide does expand the choices open concerning one's own life, but it doesn't help much concerning the harms of the world. We may be able to break whatever links there might be between ourselves and the harms through the act of suicide, but the harms will normally be unaffected by this act.

It is useful in this context to reflect on several of the writings of Jean-Paul Sartre, surely a much more theoretically oriented philosopher than Camus. In *Being and Nothingness*, Sartre puts forth his famous and widely criticized view of "absolute responsibility":

> The essential consequence of our earlier remarks is that man being condemned to be free carries the weight of the whole world on his shoulders, he is responsible for the world and for himself as a way of being.[7]

Remarks like these have led many commentators to suggest that Sartre cannot have anything like a concept of *moral* responsibility in mind in these passages, since moral responsibility for an evil world would seem to entail that each person is guilty for every harm in the world, whether that person could have had influence over those harms or not.

Let us take a look at one example Sartre uses to illustrate one's absolute responsibility.

> If I am mobilized in a war, this war is *my* war; it is in my image and I deserve it. I deserve it first because I could always get out of it by suicide or desertion; these ultimate possibles are those which must always be present for us

21

when there is a question of envisaging a situation. For lack of getting out of it, I have *chosen* it. This can be due to inertia, to cowardice in the face of public opinion, or because I prefer certain other values to the value of the refusal to join in the war. . . . Any way you look at it, it is a matter of choice.[8]

This example is similar to what Karl Jaspers says about those Germans who "fail to do whatever" they can to prevent war crimes, "without chance of success, and therefore to no purpose."[9] Just as killing oneself or deserting was not likely to end the war, so sacrificing oneself when confronted with Nazi atrocities was not likely to bring an end to those atrocities. But these are acts one can *choose* to perform which would cut the ties between the individual person and the war. In these wartime examples, there is a recognition of the social dimension, although not as much as can be found in Sartre's later writings. Neither Sartre nor Jaspers would support the principle that one is morally obligated to end one's life when faced with the possibility of being associated with a war. Indeed Jaspers explicitly says, "There is no moral obligation to sacrifice one's life in the sure knowledge that nothing will have been gained."[10] One is not normally responsible for a war in a way that leads to moral blame. Rather, what one is responsible for is the way one reacts to that war, and here again we are back to personal responsibility for self.

For the early Sartre, radical freedom is largely a thesis about the self rather than a thesis about one's ability to affect the world. We can get a better glimpse of this by considering an even more extreme example. Sartre says:

> I am ashamed of being born or I am astonished at it or I rejoice over it, or in attempting to get rid of my life I affirm that I live and I assume this life as bad. Thus, in a certain sense I *choose* being born. This choice itself is integrally affected with facticity since I am not able not to choose. . . . [11]

This analysis is similar to Jaspers's analysis of what he calls one's metaphysical guilt for simply being alive. (I address this concept in great detail in chapter 8.) The choice here is not one that a person could have avoided, and hence it is a choice that was not behaviorally under the person's control. Rather, as Jaspers points out, one chooses in "individual solitude" to transform one's "approach to the world."[12] This is a matter of attitude and character rather than of ex-

22

plicit behavior. One cannot choose not to have been born, but one can choose an attitude toward the circumstances of one's birth. As will become apparent, I endorse some of this analysis but take exception with the individualistic orientation that undergirds it.

Before turning our attention to social existentialism, let us briefly consider a very early passage in *Being and Nothingness*, in which Sartre claims that one must recognize both the reflective and pre-reflective realms of consciousness.

> This reply aims not only at the instantaneous consciousness which I can achieve by reflection but at those fleeting consciousnesses which have passed without being reflected-on, those which are forever not-reflected-on in my immediate past. Thus reflection has no kind of primacy over the consciousness reflected-on. It is not reflection which reveals the consciousness reflected-on to itself. Quite the contrary, it is the non-reflective consciousness which renders the reflection possible; there is a pre-reflective cogito which is the condition of the Cartesian cogito.[13]

Sartre's general insight about attitudes such as bad faith is that as long as we are at least pre-reflectively aware of having a given attitude, then that attitude is enough under our control for us to be responsible for it. This sets the stage for saying that we are personally responsible for virtually all of our attitudes. For if it is bad faith that makes us not fully aware of certain attitudes that we clearly have, and if we are responsible for this bad faith, then it seems that we would also be responsible for the attitudes we would deny, on a certain level of awareness, that we have.

Of equal importance, Sartre believed that we cannot be excused from responsibility for our attitudes merely because we did not choose, however painful such a choice would have been, to bring a given attitude to reflective awareness. Pre-reflective awareness of an attitude is sufficient for supporting the claim that a person could have chosen to reject that attitude, since the person could have begun such a process by first bringing the attitude before reflective awareness. Someone who holds anti-Semitic attitudes, but who denies this fact, is not relieved of responsibility for having these attitudes merely because bad faith allows him or her not to confront them reflectively.

It is important to remember that bad faith, one of the characteristics of inauthenticity, is characterized by Sartre as an "attitude" concerning a denial of consciousness of oneself.[14] One's approach to the world in bad faith is to flee the anguish that one encounters by denying what one knows, on a certain level of consciousness, about oneself and one's world.[15] But this attitude is something that is under our control. Our attitudes influence the world beyond ourselves insofar as they can often influence behavior. And it is crucial that people feel motivated to change their attitudes as a first step toward being better able to influence the world. But it is misleading to say that being able to choose our attitudes translates into responsibility for those things in the world about which we have such attitudes.

Social existentialism takes more seriously than its predecessors what is involved in changing the world. Just as early existentialists thought it was one's responsibility to come to conscious awareness of the self as a first step toward changing one's attitudes and states of mind, so later existentialists thought that it was one's responsibility to come to conscious awareness of what one can do, in combination with others, to change the world, not just to change oneself. Early existentialists, such as Camus and the early Sartre, were caught up with the isolated individual self striving to find meaning in an absurd existence. Later existentialists, such as Jaspers and the later Sartre, extended the field of inquiry to encompass the great tragedies of the world, wondering how individuals in combination rather than in isolation could have changed things. With this shift in emphasis came a shift in understanding the self and responsibility. As Jaspers put it, the change was from a "transformation of human self-consciousness before God," toward an analysis beginning with one's inner life "then also taking effect in the world of reality."[16]

In this revised notion of the responsible self, attitudes and other states of mind become most important when those attitudes are likely to increase the potential for harm or benefit in the world. And such potential cannot even be fathomed without understanding the way that individuals influence and are influenced by the communities and other groups in which significant social actions can occur. Here the ability to commit suicide is not the most important option that one has. Rather, emphasis shifts to the kinds of things that one could do, or prevent from occurring, when one acts in combination with others. Attitudes remain important for responsibility, but their importance is filtered through the gauze of what groups are capable of doing.

3. An Underground Movement in Ethics

Throughout this book, I take an existentialist perspective on moral responsibility. Existentialists have the most developed understanding of responsibility for attitudes, omissions, and social roles. They have at least a rudimentary conception of the self and of agency that would warrant the expansion of moral responsibility beyond what a person directly causes. But there have been others who have moved in the direction I suggest who have not been existentialists. Indeed, there is an underground movement to this effect that runs throughout the history of philosophy. In the next few pages I will mention some of the figures in that movement.

Greek philosophers were at least as concerned about character as they were about direct causation. As Martha Nussbaum notes, Greek moral thinking begins from

> the position of one who finds Pindar's ode anything but peculiar and who has the greatest difficulty understanding how they might ever cease to be problems. That I am an agent, but also a plant; that much that I did not make goes towards making me whatever I shall be praised or blamed for being; that I must constantly choose among competing and apparently incommensurable goods and that circumstances may force me to a position in which I cannot help being false to something or doing something wrong; that an event which simply happens to me may, without my consent, alter my life. . . .[17]

The Stoics seem to have recognized a category of moral judgment involving neither vice nor virtue. There were things that people were neither obligated to do, nor obligated not to do, and these things were called "indifferents." Even though one was not obligated to act in a certain way toward an indifferent, perhaps because it was, properly speaking unavoidable, nonetheless there were attitudes one should take toward these indifferents based on their preferability in a particular set of circumstances.[18]

In the early modern period, even though action was the key to moral responsibility, both Hobbes and Locke retained broader interests. Hobbes distinguished guilt, which is attributed to unjust actions, from unrighteousness, which is attributed to unjust people. In chapter 15 of *Leviathan* he said: "The Injustices of Manners, is the disposition or aptitude to do Injurie; and is Injustice before it proceed to Act; and without supposing any individual person injured."[19] And Locke, in discussing conquest, says that the key question of whether the members of a conquered group are guilty concerns whether they have "actually assisted, concurred or consented to that unjust force that was used against [the conqueror]."[20] By placing consent, especially tacit consent, in the center of their moral theories, these theorists at least partially participated in the underground movement to expand moral responsibility beyond that which one directly causes.

In the early part of our century, John Dewey's work is noteworthy for its emphasis on the need to "assume responsibility for continuous reconstruction of experience" as an antidote to prejudice and ignorance, which is too often responsible for irrational choices and habits.[21] Following in this spirit, various communitarians have urged that we expand our understanding of moral responsibility to one that is community-oriented. Michael Sandel has claimed that

> justice finds its occasion because we cannot know each other, or our ends, well enough to govern by the common good alone. This condition is not likely to fade altogether, and so long as it does not, justice will be necessary. But neither is it guaranteed always to predominate, and in so far as it does not, community will be possible, and an unsettling presence for justice.[22]

Most recently, Charles Taylor has sought to reorient moral thinking so that it focuses as much on our ordinary life's roles as on our conduct. Taylor identifies three axes for moral thinking: "our sense of respect for and obligations to others," "our thinking of what makes a full life," and "our dignity."

> Our "dignity," in the particular sense I am using it here, is our sense of ourselves as commanding (attitudinal) respect. . . . For instance, my sense of myself as a householder, father of a family, holding down a job, providing for my dependents; all this can be the basis for my sense of dignity.[23]

Woven into the three dimensions of a person's moral thought and life is what Taylor calls a "framework."

> Frameworks provide the background, explicit or implicit, for our moral judgments, intuitions or reactions, in any of the three dimensions. To articulate a framework is to explicate what makes sense of our moral responses.[24]

It is on the basis of such frameworks that one's identity as a distinct self is grounded. A person becomes an agent in the world because of that person's sense of self. And this means that agency arises out of these socially contextualized frameworks. For Taylor, "who one is" is as important as "what one has done" in establishing a person as an agent. One's responsibility thus also extends beyond the narrow confines of what one has directly brought about.

Finally, let me mention a group of social philosophers doing work in applied ethics who have urged that we abandon the distinction between omission and commission, as well as the distinction between being passive and being active. I am thinking of philosophers such as James Rachels, Peter Singer, and John Harris, who have argued that we have responsibilities to prevent harm where we can, regardless of whether there is anything that we have done to bring about the harmful situations in question.[25] These philosophers have urged that we expand the domain of moral responsibility in such areas as world hunger and euthanasia to make people aware that their lack of action can be as morally problematic as their direct actions. Some feminist and Black philosophers have also urged that we look at the effects of social roles on the adverse treatment of women and minorities and that we think of ourselves as responsible for specific harms against women or minorities in our cultures, even though we have not directly participated in those harms.[26]

To varying degrees, these philosophers have urged that we expand the domain of moral responsibility in similar ways to the social existentialists I have discussed. What was once an underground movement in modern moral philosophy is now becoming a groundswell. This book is an attempt to advance that position and to carry the debate about the nature of moral responsibility into new quarters. The scholarly debate has mirrored a popular one as well. Barely a week goes by without editorial essayists and politicians urging that people accept their share of responsibility for certain social problems, or urging that there is no such responsibility. In both cases, people are explicitly thinking of responsibility as potentially shared and not merely as a function of what one has directly caused on one's own.

4. Voluntariness and Involuntariness

Finally, I want to journey briefly into very recent work on moral responsibility and states of mind in mainstream analytic philosophy.

In his essay entitled "Involuntary Sins," Robert Merrihew Adams claims that people should be held responsible for various attitudes and other states of mind.[27] I agree with Adams's claim. But to reach this point Adams feels he must refute the contention that people are only responsible for what they voluntarily choose. On this point I part company with Adams. Adams argues that there is no reasonable interpretation of voluntariness that would allow such states of mind as self-righteousness to be voluntary, yet these states of mind are things for which a person is held responsible. In what follows I will argue, to the contrary, that attitudes for which people are held responsible can normally be characterized as voluntary, or at least that what makes people responsible for these states of mind has to do with something that is itself under their voluntary control.

I should say at the outset that my social existentialist account of responsibility understands a voluntary choice as a choice to bring about or not to bring about a certain effect that is based on at least partial awareness that one has a certain option. In this view, as long as it is possible to effect a change, and one is at least partially aware that one can effect this change, then not effecting it is something one has voluntarily chosen. Whatever one has under one's control, and one is at least partially aware of, is something that one either voluntarily chooses or voluntarily does not choose. Of course, as existentialists have pointed out, not choosing is also a choice.

Before examining Adams's argument, let us briefly look at an example that is supposed to render Adams's account intuitively plausible. Consider the case of anger. Adams begins his essay by pointing out that "anger is not in general voluntary." Of course, people can make voluntary efforts to control anger, but for Adams the crucial fact is that "we cannot choose to be angry or not as we normally can choose to sit or stand." Even when we are trying very hard not to be angry, indeed even when we have learned "to suppress conscious episodes of anger by redirecting our attention, we may still be profoundly affected by an unconscious anger" over which we lack control.[28] If this unconscious anger is unjust then we may be responsible for it, in Adams's account, even though it is involuntary.

Yet it seems to me that this example does not well illustrate the thesis that people are held responsible for involuntary states of mind. For people can exercise control over states of mind such as anger, at least indirectly through the intervention of psychotherapy, for instance. And it is rare indeed that a person is fully unconscious of his or her anger, in any event. It is much more likely that a person is semi-consciously aware of anger; when we blame the person for anger it is for failing to attend to his or her internal states and for failing to take action to change states that are potentially harmful.

It is true that we cannot control our attitudes and emotions with the same ease as we control whether we stand or sit. But states of mind are often enough under our control that they are, for that reason, things for which we are held responsible. And if these states of mind really are not under control, then it is not reasonable to hold people responsible for them. In fact, Adams and I agree about the disposition of most cases; what is at issue is the reason why people are indeed held responsible for some of their states of mind such as anger, as well as for various attitudes that they are not fully aware of having.

One of the sources of my disagreement with Adams concerns his analysis of a person who is self-righteous. Adams correctly points out that the "offense of the self-righteous person is typically not in what he voluntarily chooses to do, but in the motivation or attitude with which he usually does what he ought to do." Such a person has not chosen to have the motive or attitude of self-righteousness. Adams goes on to suggest, though, that what is morally wrong, and worthy of blame, is that this person "had the motive in the first place."[29] Now it may be that there is something morally wrong about the sheer possession of bad motives and attitudes, but it seems to me that for these to be blameworthy there must be a sense in which they have been chosen.

The sheer having of an attitude "in the first place" is not necessarily something a person is responsible for. If the person has been hypnotized and presented with a posthypnotic suggestion that would engender self-righteousness, this attitude may be morally bad since self-righteousness is likely to lead to harm. But, as I will argue below, it cannot be seriously alleged that the person is responsible for his or her self-righteousness. What would make ascriptions of responsibility appropriate is the extent to which a person brought this attitude upon himself or herself, or failed to take steps to prevent the engendering of the attitude.

The illicit move that Adams makes is well illustrated in the following passage:

> If someone says to me that I am incapable of feeling gratitude, or that I do not sincerely care about my moral character, or that although I act rightly I do so only because I think it the most effective way to get what I want

from other people, this claim about my feeling or motives is already an ethical indictment; and if it is true, I stand condemned.[30]

The mistake Adams makes is to assume that the obvious wrongness of a certain state of mind indicts the person, making the person blameworthy for that state. To the contrary, though, all that follows from the obvious wrongness of a state of mind is that that state of mind is indictable. Consider the possibility that a person could be born with a malicious disposition, and that it is obvious to everyone that the disposition is wrong. But it would not be intuitively plausible to say that the person who has this disposition is bad in the sense that he or she is to be blamed for having this disposition. Adams seems to believe that merely having a mental state is sufficient for that state being one's responsibility. Such a view might well be called the "possessive theory of responsibility." But until the very end of his essay it remains a mystery why possession should be the main criterion of responsibility. And when reasons are advanced, voluntariness reemerges as the basis of Adams's view.

Adams argues that if people do not recognize their own responsibility for states of mind, they will not struggle against them and ultimately not repent for having them.[31] Theological issues aside, I agree with Adams that it is important for people to struggle against dispositions they may have acquired through no fault of their own. But it seems to me that the appropriate way to do this is to hold a person responsible for failing to attempt to change a harm-producing disposition. From a social existentialist perspective, it is the way that one's states of mind contribute to social harms that is key. It matters less what one can do about these states of mind at the moment than what sort of plan one can initiate now to bring about changes in these states of mind later. Adams, though, wants us to hold people responsible for the fact that they have these dispositions. I don't think that repentance will be the response to being told that one is to blame for something one could not have prevented. Instead, the response is likely to be despair, which will not bring about a struggle against the harm-producing disposition.

A related difficulty concerns Adams's definition of voluntariness:

> To say that something is (directly) within my voluntary control is to say that I would do it (right away) if and only if I (fully) tried or meant to do so, and hence that if I did it I

> would do it *because* I tried or chose or meant to do it, and
> in that sense voluntarily.[32]

In this view, anything which is complicated enough to take time to produce is not under a person's direct voluntary control. If it takes me twenty minutes to construct a solution to a math problem, that solution is not under my direct voluntary control, since I could not have produced it immediately. Surely this is mistaken. Adams's view of direct voluntary control is defective in placing too much emphasis on what can be accomplished "right away." There are important implications of this defect for Adams's argument. Most notably, Adams fails to appreciate how habits are voluntary, and how changing our habits can, over time, give us control over a large range of our seemingly involuntary mental states. I will say much more about this in subsequent chapters (especially chapter 3).

Of crucial importance is Adams's contention that voluntariness requires conscious awareness.

> For one of the definitive marks of the voluntary is that if one does something voluntarily one knows that one is doing it. The tradition that attaches blame exclusively to the voluntary has therefore accepted ignorance as an excuse. It has not blamed us for doing things if we did not know that we were doing them or did not know that they were wrong.[33]

This is indeed the standard way that voluntariness is understood, and it is fraught with the problems that Adams has identified. But there is another account of voluntariness that is not tied to conscious awareness. As I explained above, following Sartre we should say that what is important is that people are at least pre-reflectively aware of their mental states, and that such awareness is sufficient to say that people are conscious enough of their options to call them voluntary.

One of Adams's final examples concerns the attitude of ethical sensitivity.[34] Sensitivity is a meta-level virtue for Adams; people are conscious enough of the morally relevant aspects of their surroundings, or they should be conscious enough, to be able to respond appropriately. I discuss sensitivity in much greater detail in chapter 3. What is of interest at the moment is that, for Adams, it is not required that people consciously recognize the wrongness of their acts or states of mind. Rather it is sufficient that "the data to which we are responding be rich enough to *permit* recognition of the relevant values."[35]

But it appears that Adams has here set the stage for the rejection of his own view. When people fail to be sensitive even though the data are rich enough, it is their failure that we blame, based on the assumption that they are at least pre-reflectively aware of their surroundings but that they simply aren't choosing to pay enough attention to bring it to conscious awareness. To see this point, think of someone who is insensitive due to hypnosis. Such cases of insensitivity are not blamed; rather, only those cases of insensitivity are blamed which a person could influence. Here, we are not lost in the morass of involuntary mental states, but mental states that are at least partially voluntary insofar as people *could* have chosen, and should have chosen, to pay more attention as part of a project to change those mental states in the future. They are blamed not because they simply aren't paying attention, but because they could and should have paid attention.

Adams says that "if one does something voluntarily one knows that one is doing it."[36] Initially it is not clear how to adapt this statement to the case of a person's attitudes. Would Adams maintain that if one voluntarily has an attitude then one knows that one has it? Unfortunately, our mental states often do not admit of knowledge in the same way that our external behavior does. There are many levels of awareness, but only the most self-conscious involve knowledge. Yet, there are semi-conscious attitudes (such as pre-reflective awareness) that we have some control over, in the sense that we can bring these attitudes to conscious awareness and we can then exert influence on them. For this reason it is appropriate to ascribe responsibility for these attitudes, even though we do not necessarily have knowledge of them.

Consider an example of a stereotypic attitude: a negative attitude toward women held by a middle-aged man. Because of the influence of stereotypes, this person may not be sensitive enough to his own environment to be fully aware of the potential for harm that his attitudes have. Yet if he is aware at some level of consciousness that he has these attitudes and that they can cause harm, and if he can set in motion a plan to change them, then he will have enough of an awareness to be responsible for them. Of course, such a plan may involve other people; for instance, he might enlist others to help him bring these attitudes to full conscious awareness through some sort of psychotherapy. But until brought to full conscious awareness, it is not an attitude about which the person *knows* much at all. The key to moral responsibility is not knowledge but control, which is itself the key to voluntariness.

Adams has set the stage, as he partially admits, for a return to the importance of voluntariness in responsibility ascriptions. He admits that the ability of a person to influence his or her state of mind is the key. But since this ability is often not something with an intentional object (something explicitly aimed at), he wants us to consider some states of mind that cause harm to be involuntary (because they involve mere desires, which are not intentional mental states, as opposed to choices proper). But this is only to admit that self-control is the key to responsibility; and this is traditionally what is meant by voluntariness. So while I follow Adams in thinking that people should be seen as morally responsible for their attitudes and other states of mind, I do not agree that this premise calls for the abandonment of the central role of voluntariness in our conceptualization of moral responsibility. I will take up these themes in greater detail in chapters 2 and 3.

Finally, let us consider one criticism often offered against views such as mine that seek to increase the realm of moral responsibility to include states of mind and character traits. It has become commonplace to say that the demands of morality are too restrictive in the lives of individuals.[37] Since I am urging that we extend the domain of moral responsibility further than is normally allowed, it would seem that my proposal swims against a strong contemporary current in ethics toward a minimal morality. Understood in terms of justice, it is often said that we risk weakening the fabric of our rule-following society if we too greatly burden people with obligations (such as the obligation to sacrifice one's privileged economic position so that others can have enough food to eat). Justice should demand only a reasonable minimum, so it is claimed, and it certainly should not call for people to engage in great sacrifices.[38] For if justice was understood to grant us significant claims on one another's lives, people would rebel against the institutions associated with justice, most significantly the law.

Some other moral theorists argue that there is a domain of morality, a domain that does not make demands, where there is room for speaking of the expanded considerations that people should take into account. Virtue is thought to be a different moral concept from justice, in that it concerns ideals that people should aspire toward, not only in terms of behavior but also in terms of the kind of character traits one has.[39] Such moral considerations encompass all that is nonbinding, but that is nonetheless good to do or be. People should, in an ideal world, sacrifice to aid those who are starving, but in the actual world it would merely be virtuous of them to do so. Yet such strategies seem not to capture the fact that many people think there is something wrong with not going to the aid of the hungry.

The concept of responsibility does not neatly fit the division of justice-oriented obligations and virtue-oriented ideals. Like justice, responsibility is thought to generate moral requirements. Like virtue, responsibility often concerns who one is and not just the effects of the intentional actions one has taken in the world. Responsibility, like justice, is sometimes backward-looking, concerning the harms (personal as well as social) that one has caused or the harms that one could have prevented. But responsibility, like virtue, is also forward-looking, concerning the character traits, attitudes, and dispositions that one needs to develop to minimize future harm.

The moral requirements which attach to responsibility are not free-floating in the way in which many people describe virtues. Rather they are triggered by specific facts, for example: the fact that one did or did not contribute to a group effort that ended in harm; the fact that one occupied a certain role as neighbor, citizen, philosopher; the fact that one shares with others various character traits that one could have changed and that are likely to produce harm. Of course, responsibility also attaches to very specific acts of individual persons. But while this is the model of responsibility used in legal theory, it is so used misleadingly because, unlike justice, responsibility is not predominantly an individualistic notion. Rather, responsibility has more to do with how people fit into a larger social context than it does with what individuals owe to each other as their due (the way justice is traditionally characterized).

We tend to equate moral responsibility with blame or guilt and hence to think of responsibility as not much different from legal liability. But guilt is only the most extreme form of responsibility. Guilt and blame lie at the end of a continuum which also contains shame, remorse, regret, and feeling tainted. Some of these nonguilt types of responsibility are best understood communally rather than individualistically. There are almost always degrees of nonguilt types of responsibility, whereas a person is either guilty or not guilty. Perhaps it is not too misleading to say that responsibility concerns both perfect and imperfect duties. Guilt and blame are at the end of the responsibility spectrum that parallels perfect duty, but there are other moral categories, like shame and feeling tainted, that are at the end of the responsibility spectrum that parallels imperfect duty. Just as our relationships with others are multitudinous and wide-ranging, so is the domain of responsibility.

TWO

Shared Responsibility and Racist Attitudes

At large state universities like the one where I used to teach, there has been an increase in racism. Not only have racial epithets been scrawled on bathroom stalls, but cross burnings and other more violent acts of racism are again occurring. Over the last ten years there has been a steady rise in racist attitudes among white students, faculty, and administrators. Yet the response of members of these academic communities to racially motivated violence is often to say that they do not share in responsibility for these events since they have played no causal role in the incidents. On February 4, 1988, Steven Beering, president of Purdue University, issued a public statement which read, in part: "The recent cross-burning incident at the Black Cultural Center was outrageous and deplorable. It brings shame to the responsible person, but we must not allow it to bring shame to our community."[1] This is a common response to incidents of racism in America. The individuals who directly perpetrated a harmful act are held to be responsible, to be worthy of shame, but the members of the community, many of whom share the attitudes of the perpetrators, are not held to share in the responsibility. I want to investigate the conceptual legitimacy of claiming that a person shares responsibility for harms that he or she has not directly caused, especially harms that are correlated with certain kinds of attitudes.

In this chapter I will first set out the argument for expanding the notion of responsibility to include shared responsibility for some of those things for which we are not the direct cause.[2] The cases I will examine include instances in which a person chooses to conspire with, fails to prevent, or endorses the actions of others that directly cause harm. Each of these cases involves a choice that contributed to a harm for which that person was then at least partially responsible. In the last two sections I consider the more difficult case of sharing in an attitude which leads some others to the production of a harm.

This is no longer a choice involving a doing, strictly so called, but it does involve the kind of risk of harmful behavior that is similar to some of the other cases, especially omissions and endorsements. I here set the stage for thinking that responsibility should not be narrowly confined to what a person *does,* for one's attitudes often are as important to the increased likelihood of harm in a community as one's overt behavior.

After some preliminary remarks on the nature of shared responsibility in section 1, I will discuss three different sorts of case exemplifying shared responsibility. I will begin by considering cases (in section 2) in which a person has played a causal role, although a minor one, in a joint venture. It is sometimes claimed in law that in these cases it is legitimate to hold each participant wholly responsible for what has occurred, especially if it is difficult to apportion responsibility by the extent of participation. I will challenge this model of responsibility by defending an alternative model that assigns partial rather than full responsibility for participation in a joint venture. I will then proceed to a second set of cases (in section 3) involving negligent omission or risky behavior involving harm. In some of these cases, a person's omission or risky behavior can easily be treated as if it were part of a joint venture, and responsibility can be apportioned according to the extent of contribution to the venture, even though this contribution seemed to be passive rather than active. In other cases, a person's omission or risk could have, but did not, contribute to a harmful event, yet the similar behavior of others did cause harm. I will argue that it seems reasonable to say that certain of the risk takers share in responsibility for the harms that occurred. I will consider examples (in section 4) in which a person shares with others in a community attitudes that support harmful practices in the community. I argue that even those who do not directly produce the relevant harms may nonetheless share in responsibility for them because of sharing the attitudes that support these practices. A consideration of these examples will allow us to see the need to expand the limits of agent causation in cases involving shared responsibility, a topic which I briefly address in the final section of the chapter.

1. The Concept of Shared Responsibility

The cases I am concerned to analyze involve situations where it seems to make sense to divide responsibility among the members of a group, rather than to hold each member fully responsible or to hold the whole group collectively responsible. To say that the members of a group share in responsibility for a harm is different from saying that a group is collectively responsible for a given harm.[3] When a group of people shares responsibility for a harm, responsibility distributes to each member of the group. When a group is collectively responsible for a harm, the group as such is responsible; but this does not necessarily mean that all, or even any, of the members are individually responsible for the harm. Collective responsibility refers to a form of nondistributional responsibility in which some feature of the group facilitates collective action thereby rendering the group's actions more than merely the sum of the actions of the members of the group. Shared responsibility does not depend on the existence of a cohesive group since it concerns only aggregated personal responsibility.

Dividing responsibility for a harm is also different from assigning to each of several people full responsibility for a harm. Some or all members of a group may be assigned less than full responsibility for a harm in cases of divided or shared responsibility. When a person is assigned less than full responsibility for a harm, that person still is subject to blame, punishment, or shame for what has occurred, and should feel motivated to choose differently in the future, just as in a case of full individual responsibility. But, unlike full individual responsibility, shared responsibility calls attention to the way in which the actions or attitudes of a group of people resulted in a harm; that is, attention is focused on the way in which each of us interacts with others, rather than on the individual person as an isolated agent.

I conceive of shared responsibility from a social existentialist perspective. Here the idea is that it is our choices, rather than what we actually do, or even can do, that is important. Emphasis is placed as much on the attitudes we choose to have, or choose to endorse, as it is on our outward behavior. If we focus only on personal responsibility for what we fully control, proper attention is not given to the fact that many people contribute indirectly to a harm, or that many people have the same attitudes and dispositions as the people who cause harm. These people may share responsibility for the harms, as I will argue below, even though they do not have full control over the harms.

In moral and legal theory it is often claimed that someone is personally responsible for a harm if that person directly produced that harm through an intentional act or through negligence. A person is the direct (or proximate) cause of some harmful event if that person's voluntary behavior was part of a causal chain that produced the harmful event, and if no other person's voluntary behavior occurred later in the causal chain and was necessary for that harmful event.[4] In both moral and legal theory it is often claimed that if someone played no causal role in producing a harm, that person is not responsible for that harm. In this model, people can only be said to share in responsibility for a harm to the extent they directly contributed to the harm.

When two or more people engage in a joint action that produces harm, the model of individual personal responsibility fails to be helpful. For in joint undertakings the causal contribution of each person often cannot easily be ascertained, except to say that all parties played a necessary causal role in the harm, and that no one party played a sufficient role. Because the participation of each was necessary, it seems appropriate to assign some responsibility to each participant. But since no one party's participation was sufficient to produce the harm, it seems inappropriate to assign full responsibility to one party. A person's participation does not give good guidance for determining how individual responsibility should be assigned in such cases, as we will see in section 2. This is one reason for talking of shared rather than individual responsibility in such cases.

In addition to joint action, there are two other cases in which shared rather than individual full responsibility seems appropriate. First, a person's action may have been voluntary and even intentional and yet committed with no knowledge or intent of contributing to a harm. But it may nonetheless be true that the person did perform a necessary part in a harm and thereby implicated herself or himself partially in the harm that resulted. Insofar as a person did choose a behavior or attitude that contributed to harm, it makes sense to hold the person partly responsible for the harm, even though it may not make sense to hold the person fully responsible for the harm. (I will consider this issue in discussing cases of omissions in section 3.) A person who engages in such behavior should not be assigned the same degree of responsibility as a person who intends to contribute to a joint action to cause harm.

There are situations in which a person who did not directly cause a harm nevertheless acted so as to increase the risk of the occurrence of harm. (I will examine these cases in detail in sections 3 and 4.) This sort of behavior seems to exemplify a lesser degree of responsibility than that resulting from directly harmful action. Assigning partial responsibility for the harm may be just the right compromise between full responsibility and no responsibility at all. Notice that when people do not feel responsible at all (for having played necessary but minor roles in the harm or for merely increasing the likelihood that the harm would occur), they will generally not seek to change their behavior. Employing the notion of shared responsibility in such cases allows people to view their degree of responsibility as significant enough to take their potential roles in harm seriously.

The burden of this chapter is to show that there are good reasons to expand the range of conditions on the basis of which we may say that someone shares responsibility for a harm. I will argue that in some cases of conspiracy, omission, risk, and racism, people share responsibility for harms that other people have directly caused. In doing so, as I explain in detail in the final section of the chapter, I remain committed to the idea that responsibility should be connected to agency, that is, to what one has personally and freely chosen.

2. Joint Ventures and Conspiracies

As early as the beginning of the seventeenth century it was a well-established principle of English (and later American) legal theory that those who act in concert with others are each personally liable for harms caused by their concerted action. The leading hornbook on torts, written by Prosser and Keaton, asserts:

> The original meaning of a "joint tort" was that of vicarious liability for concerted action. All persons who acted in concert to commit a trespass, in pursuance of a common design, were held liable for the entire result. . . . Each was therefore liable for the entire damage done, although one might have battered, while the other imprisoned the plaintiff, and a third stole the plaintiff's silver buttons.[5]

Indeed, in a footnote to this text, Prosser and Keaton add that "it makes no difference that the damage inflicted by one tortfeasor exceeds what the others might reasonably have foreseen."[6]

The person who battered down the plaintiff's door did not take the silver buttons; and the same may be said of the person who restrained the plaintiff. Yet, each of these people is held personally responsible for having stolen the plaintiff's silver buttons. Each is treated in the same manner as the person who actually took the buttons. Since each of the members of a conspiracy perform actions that play necessary roles in the joint undertaking, it seems reasonable to hold each at least partially responsible for the injurious act. But in common law it was held, even more strongly, that each party was *fully* responsible for stealing the buttons.

Joint ventures involving concerted action are treated differently in law from other kinds of joint ventures. Concerted action requires first of all some sort of tacit understanding or agreement among the parties. But such an understanding is not reached when there is "mere knowledge by each party of what the other was doing."[7] Rather, in addition, there must be one clearly recognized goal (or set of goals) toward which each sees their actions as directed. Also, the overall venture must incorporate each person's action in such a way that it is not practically possible to measure the extent of each person's contribution simply by analyzing the joint venture into its constituent parts (as we can see in examining the disparate acts of breaking open the door, restraining the plaintiff, and rifling the plaintiff's jewelry box). When these conditions are met then each party is responsible in law for all of the harm caused by the joint venture.

The basis of this legal policy is that if individuals pursue a common plan for a common gain in such a way that it is not easy to separate the role and gain of each from that of the others, then each is guilty for all of the harms done in pursuit of the common gain.[8] In normal cases of individual agency, a person is considered responsible only for those effects he or she has personally brought about. If a person causes only part of a harm, then he or she should be considered responsible only for that part. But for some joint ventures such a strategy for assigning responsibility is not workable in practice. In the case of the plaintiff's silver buttons, the part of the harm each conspirator caused to the plaintiff is difficult to determine if we focus on the isolated acts, such as battering down the plaintiff's door. It is not clear how large or small a part in the harm of stealing the plaintiff's buttons was played by the act of battering down the door. It is thus not clear, on the model of individual agency, what the door batterer should be considered personally responsible for, other than the broken door itself. This practical problem of measuring partial responsibility is the reason why the legal tradition considers each participant in a joint venture responsible for all of the harm. Yet surely there are other alternatives.

In such cases of joint action, there are at least three possibilities. Responsibility could be divided, either evenly or unevenly, based on who played the most or least significant role in leading the group; the harm would be divided into parts and each participant would be assigned some but not all responsibility for the harm. As I've indicated, I prefer the uneven-division variation of this strategy. The two other ways of dealing with the situation are to assign none of the responsibility to each person, since none of them fully caused the harm, or to assign full responsibility to each person, as in the original law case from the seventeenth century. Of course, none of these strategies follows the normal model of individual agency mentioned at the beginning of this chapter. That is, none of these strategies apportions responsibility based on the proportion of the causal role played by each person in the production of the harm. Because of this, each alternative constitutes a break in the normal relationship between agency and responsibility.

It is not sufficiently appreciated that the way Anglo-American law has treated conspiracies and joint ventures is at odds with the normal model of individual agency. People are held personally and even fully responsible for effects they only partially caused. The way that the law has treated conspiracies and joint ventures provides a preliminary challenge to the way the traditional model assigns responsibility. But the answer that the law framed, namely, to hold each person fully responsible regardless of that person's specific contribution to the joint undertaking, is not satisfactory. In such cases responsibility should be shared, rather than fully assigned to each person who contributes to a joint undertaking. I turn next to cases of omission and risky behavior to explore further the variety of examples of shared responsibility. These cases show, more clearly than the cases of joint undertaking we have just examined, what is wrong with assigning full individual responsibility to each person who contributes to harms perpetrated by the combined actions (or inactions) of more than one person.

3. Omissions and Risks

Negligent omissions concern things left undone that a person had a duty to do. Those who have such duties are responsible for their omissions in ways not true of other people who omitted the same actions but had no duty to do them. The salesperson who sold you your car and omitted to warn you about the danger of operating it in a certain way may well be responsible for the harm resulting from your operating it in that way, even though such harm was not intended by the salesperson and the salesperson's behavior did not directly produce the harm. On the other hand, if I as your neighbor omitted to warn you about the danger of operating your car in that particular way, my omission is not connected to your harm in the way that the car salesperson's is, since I do not stand in a special relationship with you.

Omissions can facilitate and even enhance the ability of others to do certain kinds of things. If I have been designated to supervise your conduct, it will take an omission on my part to allow you to act in ways that my supervisory veto could have negated. By omitting to block your proposed action, I facilitate your behavior, and my action is similar to my contribution to a type of joint venture. Consider a case in which I am supposed to supervise your operation of a forklift truck on a loading dock. If after giving the keys to you, I leave the premises, then any harm caused by your use of the forklift truck is a harm that I facilitated as supervisor. When it is true that I have a supervisory duty to block certain of your actions, then my omitting to block your action is similar to my contribution to a joint venture. Hence, it is commonly recognized in law and morality that those who fail in their supervisory duties share in responsibility for harms resulting from such omissions.

When a person's negligent omission contributes to the production of a harmful effect, then it is reasonable to consider that person to be partly responsible for that harm. The reason is that negligent omissions create a situation in which there is much greater likelihood that harmful effects will be produced. Negligence generally creates risks because due care is not being exercised in the prevention of harm. Negligent omissions are a kind of risky behavior even when no harm is actually produced. In all such cases, it does not make much sense to assign full responsibility to each participant since the roles of the participants vary so greatly. Also, negligent omissions do not clearly contribute to a discrete part of the harmful result.

Let us turn now to three cases of risky behavior, in an attempt to assess the plausibility of the claim that risk takers should share in responsibility for certain harms even though their behaviors and attitudes do not directly cause these harms. First of all, consider the case of someone who does not remove the snow from his sidewalk, knowing that his omission risks harm to delivery people; in fact one such person slips and hurts himself. Even if there is no intent to bring about the harm, it is generally thought that the taking of a risk itself renders a person responsible for any harms reasonably expected to follow from the risky omission or commission. This is a key assumption for my analysis and one quite commonly recognized. Such a premise is recognized in tort and criminal law. Certain risk takers are considered liable for various harms because of their recklessness, even though the harm is an unintended consequence of their behavior.

Consider next the case of two people, each of whom does not remove the snow from his or her portion of a common sidewalk, although each knows that harm to delivery people and others is risked. The first person's omission actually results in an accident on his portion of the sidewalk; the second person's omission does not result in harm. If both displayed the same knowledgeability and lack of due care, then the first person is unlucky and the second is lucky. And in law only one, the first person, will have his omission viewed as legally actionable, since only on his portion of the sidewalk was there any harm to be remedied. But it seems that both are at fault for having knowingly engaged in a risky enterprise. From a moral perspective, as I will argue below, both people have engaged in risky omissions, and the fact that one of them was unlucky does not seem relevant.[9] One party may be more guilty than the other, but neither should be fully relieved of responsibility for the harm.

As is well known, one of the problems with allowing luck to be considered morally relevant is that a person's moral responsibility then turns on a factor which is completely beyond the control of the person in question. I will later argue for expanding the range of things for which it is relevant to hold people morally responsible, in particular to our attitudes and beliefs. But in arguing for the view that the attitudes and beliefs we choose, not just our overt behaviors, are relevant to judgments of responsibility, I remain committed to the view that people should only be judged morally responsible for those things that are under their control; but control does not necessarily mean that one could have made the world a different place. Here it remains true that whether one shoveled one's part of the sidewalk or not, the harm on the other part would still have occurred.

The importance of stressing control in moral responsibility is that it correctly puts the emphasis on what people have chosen (to do or to be). But if it should be true, in the cases we are here considering, that a person is relieved of responsibility merely due to good luck, even though her choices are faulty, then the notion of being a moral agent, which includes our choices of who we are and not just of what we do, ceases to have the high moral importance it is normally afforded. I'll return to this point in the final section of this chapter.

Consider finally the case of someone who owns a portion of a common sidewalk and who observes another person fail to remove the snow from his portion of the sidewalk. The first person then sees that a delivery person is harmed by this omission. Having made this observation, during the next snowstorm the observer nonetheless then decides not to remove the snow from her portion of the sidewalk. Again, due to good luck, the observer's action does not result in harm, even though the similar behavior of another neighbor does result in harm. Yet it seems that the observer is perhaps even more at fault than the person whose behavior resulted in harm. The observer has engaged in omissions in a way that she has already observed to produce harm. Such behavior is best described as morally reckless and probably also blameworthy.

Yet the reckless observer's behavior did not seem to contribute to the perpetration of a harmful result at all. Indeed, it might be claimed that since no harm was produced there is no causal responsibility for harm either. It thus seems odd to say that the reckless observer is morally at fault, since there is no harm of which this person is even partially causally responsible. However, the reckless observer did initiate a causal process that she recognized as likely to result in harm, even though the causal process did not actually result in harm. Following the model of criminal law we might think of this act as involving an attempted harm. In order to be at fault (or guilty) of an attempted harm a person must knowingly initiate a causal process which is likely to produce harm.

It is my contention that those who knowingly risk harm to others, even when their behavior does not directly cause any harm, share responsibility for the harm caused by those whose similar actions directly produce that harm. The reason for this is quite straightforward: the person who merely risks harm and the person who risks *and* actually causes harm have both acted in morally similar ways. When two people both have increased the likelihood of harm and both are equally knowledgeable that their actions increased the likelihood of harm, then their risky behavior creates a greater likelihood than previously existed that harm will occur, and they should share in the responsibility for the harms that result. In the remainder of this chapter I will expand on one particular sort of risk taking, namely, contributing to a climate of racist attitudes in a community.

4. Racist Attitudes and Risks

Various attempts can lead to an increased likelihood of harm. For example, a parent's careless attitude regarding the safety of his children can easily lead to behavior likely to produce harm. Such a careless attitude could lead the parent to operate a car in an area where his children are playing, thereby increasing the likelihood that the automobile will strike and harm one of the children. But the attitude of carelessness can also increase the risk of harm by others. The careless parent is likely to omit taking various precautions, such as removing rusty objects and matches from proximity to children's toys; he thereby increases the likelihood that children would harm themselves.

In discussing potentially harmful attitudes, I am not interested in what may be described as *mere* thoughts. Attitudes are not mere cognitive states, but they are also affective states in which a person is, under normal circumstances, moved to behave in various ways as a result of having a particular attitude. The test for whether someone actually has a particular attitude or not is a behavioral test, or at least a counterfactual behavioral analysis, based on the assumption that if a person really does have a certain attitude, then certain behavior normally results. In this section, I will discuss cases in which a person has an attitude likely to result in harm, in situations in which others with similar attitudes are causing harm.

Certain cultural attitudes, such as racism, can have an effect similar to that produced by the careless parent. Those who have racist attitudes, as opposed to those who do not, create a climate of attitudes in which harm is more likely to occur. We come now to the central applied concern of this chapter, namely, to show that the members of a community who share racist attitudes also share in responsibility for racially motivated harms produced by some of the members because of this climate of racist attitudes. Here is a more extreme case of sharing responsibility for effects one has not directly caused than those previously discussed. Indeed, in the case of cultural racism, it may happen that only a small number of the members of such a community directly perpetrate harm, yet most or all of the members share in responsibility for these harms.

The members of a group who hold racist attitudes, both those who have directly caused harm and those who could directly cause harm but haven't done so yet, share in responsibility for racially motivated harms in their communities by sharing in the attitude that risks harm to others. Consider again the case of racial violence on college campuses. When administrators and faculty condone racist attitudes, sometimes adopting those attitudes themselves, a risk of racial violence is created. The individual racist attitudes considered as an aggregate constitute a climate of attitude and disposition that increases the likelihood of racially motivated harm. The climate of racist attitudes creates an atmosphere in which the members of a community become risk takers concerning racial violence.[10]

My thesis is that insofar as people share in the production of an attitudinal climate, they participate in something like a joint venture that increases the likelihood of harm. Those who hold racist attitudes, but who do not themselves cause harm directly, participate in the racial harms of their societies in two distinct ways: first, by causally contributing to the production of racial violence by others; and second, by becoming, like the reckless observer discussed above, people who choose to risk harm and yet do nothing to offset this risk. I will take up each of these points in turn.

First, those who hold racist attitudes may participate in racial violence by causally contributing to a climate that influences others to cause harm. There are several distinct ways in which having contributed to a climate of opinion may make a person responsible for the harms perpetrated by others who are influenced by that climate. In some cases there may be a straightforward causal connection between those who contribute to a climate of opinion and those who perpetrate a harm. Think of Thomas Becket, archbishop of Canterbury, who was murdered by Henry II's knights after the king created a climate of opinion simply by asking aloud why he had no followers loyal enough to rid him of the false priest. Here one person's expressed attitudes created in others a hatred that causally contributed to a harm, just as if that person had contributed to a common undertaking. Henry II's attitudes, once publicly known, had a strong impact on the attitudes and behaviors of the members of his court. Even though Henry did not direct his knights to murder Thomas (and may not have intended that his behavior be interpreted as his knights did), few would dispute that Henry shared in the responsibility for the murder of Thomas. Such judgments rely on the causal connection between Henry's attitudes and behavior and the attitudes and behavior of those who murdered Thomas.

In other cases a person's contribution to a climate of opinion has a much less straightforward causal connection with the perpetration of a harm. Consider someone who is a member of a group of people who voice public disapproval of another group of people, knowing that their acts are likely to incite still others to violence against the disapproved group. Such a person may be responsible for the harms that occur even though, due to good luck, his own public disapproval was not the act of disapproval that *directly* provoked the violence. Rather, his contribution was a bit more remote; perhaps he provided the first straw, but not the proverbial last straw that broke the camel's back. Both of these cases concern attitudes that are publicly expressed and that at least indirectly contribute to the production of harm. I turn next to situations in which the resultant harm does not depend on the public expression of racist attitudes.

The second main group of cases concerns members of a group who continue to hold racist attitudes even after similar attitudes in others are known to have produced racially motivated violence. These members share in responsibility for the racially motivated harm even if their attitudes have not been publicly expressed and have not straightforwardly contributed to the harm. If having a certain attitude leads some people to cause harm, then each person who holds that attitude risks being a producer of harm. To do that which risks harm to another, especially if it is known that the harm is highly likely and not merely possible, implicates the risk taker in these harms. And while the share in the responsibility may be greater for one who holds the risky attitude and directly causes harm than it is for one who does not directly cause harm, nonetheless there is a sharing in the responsibility for harm by all those who share the potentially harm-producing attitudes.

In some of these cases, those who hold racist attitudes should share in responsibility for racially motivated violence because their racist attitudes may reinforce, or even contribute, to the legitimation of the racist attitudes of those who do produce racially motivated violence. On college campuses, the racist attitudes of faculty members or administrators often have a clear impact on students who actually engage in racially motivated violence. Here the racist attitudes of the faculty members and administrators might stand in a causal chain, but that chain is tenuous and not normally the kind of causal contribution that makes someone responsible for a harm. What is important is *not* any direct causal connection but the fact that these attitudes indirectly contribute to a climate of opinion that makes racially motivated violence more likely. Because of this, I believe these faculty members and administrators share in responsibility for the racially motivated harms in their communities.

In other cases, those who hold racist attitudes do not *do* anything that could be said to stand in the causal chain leading to racially motivated violence. But insofar as these people do not try to decrease the chances of such violence by changing their own attitudes, given that similar attitudes in others have produced harm, they demonstrate a kind of moral recklessness, similar to that of the reckless observer, which implicates them in the racially motivated violence. In these cases, the person with racist attitudes is like someone who aims a gun at another person and pulls the trigger but, unbeknownst to him, there is no bullet in the chamber. The fact that the gun does not go off in his hands, but it does go off in the hands of the next person to pull the trigger, does not eliminate his share in the responsibility for the harm. Both people who act recklessly share responsibility not just for the risk but for the actual harm. While it is true that the one who actually caused the harm is the one who is generally taken to court, the matter is different if we are not primarily interested in choosing who is the most guilty person.

In American law there is a famous case involving a drug, DES, which was taken by pregnant women to prevent miscarriages.[11] It turned out that DES caused cancer in a number of the daughters of the women who had taken it. Because of the length of time it took for the harm to manifest itself, it was not clear in a particular woman's case which of several manufacturers had produced the dose of the drug that had caused the cancer. The court decided to apportion damages among all the manufacturers based on the likelihood that each company had produced the dose of DES in question (as determined by each company's share of the market at the time the dose was sold). The manufacturers of DES had each contributed to what had turned out to be a hazardous environment for pregnant women and their daughters. When it is unclear who actually perpetrated a harm, it seems acceptable to apportion responsibility according to likelihood of having been a harm producer. This is especially true when all the members of a group act in identical or relevantly similar ways. I want to suggest that this strategy is equally valid in some cases even when we do have knowledge of which member actually produced the harm in question. To return to the example of pulling the trigger of a partially loaded gun, someone who takes such risks with the health and safety of others should not be relieved of responsibility due to good luck, nor should all of the responsibility fall on the person who has the bad luck to pull the trigger when a bullet has come into the chamber.

It might be objected that having racist attitudes is not like pulling the trigger of a gun that may or may not be loaded.[12] Such an objection might be based on the claim that there is a significant difference between those who act on their attitudes and those who do not, which is not captured in the analogy of two people who both clearly act on the basis of their motivations. I would respond by again emphasizing that there is a difference between those who have mere thoughts or beliefs and those who have attitudes. Attitudes involve dispositions to behave in various ways. And while it is possible to override these dispositions, the cases I am considering involve those who do nothing to prevent their attitudes from leading to behavior that could cause harm. The failure to do anything to prevent one's racist attitudes from leading to racially motivated violence is similar to the failure of the person who aims a loaded gun to do anything to make sure that the gun will not go off. I take it that most people who have racist attitudes have not done anything to make sure that their attitudes do not lead them to racially motivated violence. I would agree that a person who is aware of having racist attitudes and who chooses to suppress them or to allow them to be overridden by other motivations is not like the person who pulls the trigger of a gun that may or may not be loaded. The first person's precautions against violent behavior will normally mitigate his or her responsibility.

The racist who does not directly cause harm, but who chooses to maintain unsuppressed attitudes not significantly different from those of other racists whose attitudes he or she knows, or should know, directly cause harm, should share in responsibility for the racial harms perpetrated by those in society who share the racist attitudes. The racist who directly causes harm, and those racists I have described who do not, are both responsible for racially motivated harm. The racist who does not cause harm is responsible because he or she shares in the attitudes and dispositions that, but for good luck, would cause harm.

In *On Guilt and Innocence*, Herbert Morris tries to make sense of

Karl Jaspers's claim that all Germans shared guilt for the Holocaust. Morris describes a type of shared guilt concerning

> the deeds and characteristics of others. We connect ourselves in some way with these others and when they act we see it not just reflected on them but on us. . . . We are not at fault, but we still see their conduct as reflecting on us, reflecting perhaps on deficiencies we share with them.[13]

Morris correctly identifies one of the sources of shared guilt: a feeling that another's deficiency has produced a harm and that I share this deficiency. Each person with the deficiency shares the risk of harm because each is negligent for risking the harm that the deficiency is known to have produced. The shared risk of being a harm producer is the element which links the members to the harm caused by other members.

All those who hold racist attitudes and have done nothing significant to make it less likely that they will directly cause racial violence, even though they could have, share in responsibility for that violence. This is similar to my claim about those who engage in negligent omissions. But this is not to say that all those who hold racist attitudes share to the same degree in the responsibility as all others who hold these attitudes and have also directly caused racially motivated harm as a result. Those who have not actually caused harm may often find that shame rather than blame or punishment is the proper category to describe what should follow from their sharing responsibility for various harms. Indeed it is often true that *feeling* guilty or responsible is what should properly be the response of those who have these attitudes, rather than being *held* guilty or responsible. It will also often make sense to employ categories of responsibility here that do not involve the kind of accusatory stance toward the person in question that is involved in talk of guilt or blame. This is why, I take it, Morris talks of a "deficiency" rather than a fault. I will address this point in much greater detail in chapter 8.

As I have argued, all those people who hold racist attitudes in communities where racially motivated violence occurs share in the responsibility for these harms. An important objection to what I have set out here is that my analysis of shared responsibility for racially motivated harms disconnects the notion of agency from responsibility by assigning responsibility to those who are not themselves the agents of harm. I shall end this chapter by offering a very brief response to this objection.

5. *Agency and Attitudes*

In the second and third sections of this chapter I tried to expand the limits of agency to include those types of conduct that contributed (by conspiracy or omission) to a particular result. Being directly the cause of a result may be paradigmatic for being responsible for it, but it is not, I argued, a necessary condition for being responsible for it. At the end of the third section I suggested that having a readiness to risk harm may be as appropriately a basis of responsibility for any such harm done as the harm a person directly causes. Of course, having a readiness to risk harm is often something one chooses, in the sense that it is an endorsing of a certain type of behavioral response to a situation. The importance of this endorsement becomes quite clear in the example of racism in the fourth section. For when racist attitudes are known to have precipitated racially motivated violence, anyone in a community who chooses to continue to have unsuppressed racist attitudes endorses the maintenance of a racially hazardous environment. People should be held responsible for many things for which they are not the direct cause. But to say this is not necessarily to disconnect agency from responsibility. Rather, my proposal calls for expanding the limits of agency to include those attitudes and dispositions that make overt behavior, even the behavior of others, more likely to occur.[14]

Agency should be conceived of in such a way as to include the attitudes and dispositions of those who do not directly perpetrate the act for which responsibility is in question, but whose attitudes and dispositions provide a climate that increases the likelihood these acts will be committed. People can thereby share in agency for harms they have not directly caused. It is common to discuss agency in terms of the connection between a person's own attitudes and that person's explicit behavior. What I am suggesting is that agency should not be conceived so individualistically. A person's attitudes and dispositions form a context within which that person behaves. The collection of attitudes and dispositions within a community form a climate within which individual behavior occurs. The behavior of an individual is often as deeply influenced by the climate of opinion within the individual's community as by the individual's own attitudes. Once attitudes are recognized as important components of agency, it is a mistake to focus too narrowly in discussing agency on the individual actor's own attitudes, to the exclusion of the attitudes of others who may influence the actor. I take this point up in greater detail in chapter 9.

Furthermore, individual action rarely, if ever, takes place in a moral vacuum. There are many social factors that make a particular action more likely to occur; indeed, action in the world is as much a function of groups as of individuals. Among other things, actions are made more likely to occur when there is an increase in the number of people who are inclined or disposed to so act. As I have argued, it makes sense to speak of shared agency when one person's conduct is influenced by the actions or omissions of others. Similarly, it makes sense to speak of shared agency when a climate of attitudes is created in a community that makes a given act more likely to occur. And the concept of shared agency makes sense for those cases in which a change in the climate of attitudes in a group has made it more likely that an act will be perpetrated by one of the members of that group.

Some may worry that my expansion of the concepts of agency and responsibility runs the risk of weakening the sense of personal responsibility that most people have by stretching these concepts to such an extent that they seem to demand what is unreasonable rather than what previously seemed so reasonable. I don't believe that people will respond to my proposals in this way. But even if some were to be so influenced, there is a countervailing effect that is of more importance. My proposal is part of a larger project with the aim of creating an expanded sense of group responsibility, in which individual persons come to see the extent to which their attitudes and behaviors interconnect with the attitudes and behaviors of other individual persons. In advanced technological societies, much greater evil is done by groups of persons than by discrete individual persons. And evil is made much more likely when people do not understand how failure to change their attitudes or behaviors facilitates the production of harm within the groups of which they are members. Delineating the extent to which people share responsibility for harms that occur in their groups will lead to an increased sensitivity to the role that group members could and should play in the prevention of those harms.

To sum up, shared agency, in the simplest sort of case, involves situations in which two or more people act together to produce a common result. Similarly, if one person's omission negligently creates an opportunity for another person to act harmfully, both people share in responsibility for this harm. But there can also be shared agency when one person's attitudes and beliefs (normally publicly expressed) influence another person's actions, as was the case when Henry II influenced his knights. Furthermore, shared agency can sometimes involve situations in which two or more people each choose to have attitudes or dispositions known to produce harm, but on the basis of which only one person directly causes a harm. This last case is surely the most controversial of the four, but I have tried to show that the rationale for it is quite similar to that for the other three more obvious cases of shared agency. In all of the four cases, we have shared responsibility because there is some sort of shared agency. What has happened in the final case is that our understanding of agency has expanded to encompass the less direct influences on individual behavior of the attitudes and beliefs others have chosen. When people choose to contribute to a risky or hazardous environment, such as exists when people share racist attitudes, they should share in responsibility for the harms that occur in that environment.

Insensitivity and Moral Responsibility

In this chapter I will extend further the argument advanced at the end of chapter 2 for the claim that people are responsible for various attitudes and states of mind. Specifically, this chapter considers a handful of attitudes that are all related to the concept of insensitivity. Since there has been very little philosophical work devoted to this topic, one of my first tasks in this chapter is to sketch the broad contours of the subject, noting how several traditional philosophical areas of inquiry will be affected by an investigation of insensitivity. In section 1 I provide an analysis of what it means to be sensitive, and I begin to indicate some of the morally significant ways that a person may be said to be insensitive. In section 2 I claim that sensitivity is a meta-virtue because of its unique relation to what used to be called the moral sense. In section 3 I discuss several ways that people may be morally responsible for being insensitive. Here I am guided by parallel arguments concerning physical disability and culpable ignorance. In the final two sections I take up the hard case of insensitivity caused by stereotypic beliefs and attitudes. I consider various ways in which it may be said that people are responsible for having become and remaining insensitive even when it is difficult or impossible at the moment to choose to be different.

What is meant by calling someone "an insensitive person" typically is that the person displays certain attitudes including a lack of awareness of the effects of his or her actions on others and a failure to care about these effects. The term "insensitivity" is also used to describe mere failure to notice various moral details in one's life. This usage is quite similar to the custom in contemporary art criticism of saying that someone is insensitive to detail. A person may also be said to be insensitive to his or her own attitudes and beliefs. I will say a bit about these uses at the very end of this chapter.

While there are other uses of this term, I will be mainly concerned with "insensitive responses" to the needs and feelings of others. In this sense, the term "insensitivity" is used for both mundane and rather monumental matters. A teacher shows insensitivity toward a particular student by using vulgar terminology offensive to the student. President Ronald Reagan showed insensitivity to the plight of the poor by proposing budget cuts that would have made it less likely that poor people could secure adequate food, shelter, and medical care. In the first case, insensitivity encompasses a lack of awareness of, and care for, the *feelings* of others; in the second case, insensitivity encompasses a lack of awareness of, and care for, the *needs* of others. Insensitivity can lead to the minor harms of causing offense, or it can lead to such major harms as the oppression of an entire group of people. I will try to provide a plausible account of the concepts of sensitivity and insensitivity, which will do justice to each type of case and which will set out my reasons for thinking that people should view themselves as responsible for having or lacking the attitude of sensitivity.

In analyzing sensitivity and insensitivity I will be guided by the large stock of examples of the use of these terms in ordinary speech. My analysis will attempt to provide a theoretical structure to accommodate the variety of examples. I will make one major omission, though. "Sensitivity" is sometimes used to describe someone whose own feelings are easily offended; "Don't be so sensitive" often simply means "Don't be so quick to respond emotionally to a possible slight." In my opinion, this usage is not very interesting from a moral perspective. I am interested in discussing cases of sensitivity and insensitivity that are of moral importance, and most of these concern ways people react to the needs and feelings of others.

1. The Concept of Sensitivity

In this section I will analyze the concept of moral sensitivity into four overlapping components: perceptiveness, caring, critical appreciation, and strong motivation. First of all, sensitivity involves a kind of *perceptiveness* toward the needs or feelings of others. The sensitive person is aware of, perhaps even vigilant about ascertaining, whether or not anyone will be adversely affected by his or her conduct. This does not mean, as I will explain later when considering the case of the sympathetic parent, that the sensitive person never acts so as to harm or offend. Rather, the sensitive person simply makes it his or her business to be attentive to the likely effects of his or her actions.

Iris Murdoch has noted the importance for moral attitudes and character traits of a certain type of awareness. She uses the word "'attention' . . . to express the idea of a just and loving gaze directed upon an individual reality." A person needs to observe the contexts faced by others in order to counteract what Murdoch calls the "states of illusion" or "distorted vision," which are involved when "the fat, relentless ego" pays attention only to the effects of its own actions on itself.[1] When a person's attention is fixed only on himself or herself, the self creates the illusion that the self is the only important moral concern. To overcome such self-centeredness, one must direct attention away from the self and toward the other people and things in one's world. While some parts of Murdoch's analysis are questionable, as I will explain later, she is nevertheless right to think that some type of perceiving or attending is a key ingredient in moral attitudes such as sensitivity.

Secondly, the sensitive person *cares* about the effects of his or her action. This feature of sensitivity has two aspects. The sensitive person cares about the well-being of others and will often act to advance the well-being of others. More importantly, a sensitive person generally tries to avoid conduct harmful or offensive to other persons. In both respects, the sensitive person regards the well-being of others as a very important consideration in reaching a moral judgment. The insensitive person largely lacks such a caring disposition. This does not mean that the sensitive person must always put the well-being of others ahead of his or her own well-being.[2] But a sensitive person must display more than a mere awareness of the responses of others to his or her conduct.

Consider a man who insists on paying a female business acquaintance's check at a restaurant, even though the lunch is a business lunch and the woman has complained many times about his behavior. The man considers himself to be extremely generous and also chivalrous. At least one of these traits is normally considered a virtue. And indeed, his behavior could be said to be generous, but inappropriately so. What he is missing is a sensitivity to the woman's feelings and wants, especially to her sense of autonomy and her desire for a position of professional equality with him. He may be *aware* at some level of consciousness of her feelings and wants; but if he intentionally disregards them in his conduct, he would still be insensitive, since he fails to *care* about these feelings of hers. And such an analysis does not necessarily take at face value the expressed needs and desires of others.

Thirdly, the sensitive person exercises a *critical appreciation* for what is morally relevant about the situation of those who are affected by his or her behavior. Sensitivity involves not only a caring perceptiveness of how one's actions affect others, but also the ability to discriminate normatively among the morally significant aspects of these effects. Ultimately, this can contribute to a moral judgment concerning what ought to be done.

In contrast to sensitivity, sympathy is a capacity to be affected by the suffering of others by identifying with or accepting the expressed wants of another person.[3] The sensitive person does not necessarily accept a person's expressed wants. To illustrate this point let us contrast two cases. Consider a father who always consoles his children when they are in distress. Imagine, though, that one of these children often makes unreasonable demands on peers and adults alike and is distressed when the demands are thwarted. A *sympathetic* father will suffer with his distressed child and attempt to console the child with soothing words and hugs. But a *sensitive* father will sometimes withhold consolation when he believes it necessary for the long-run developmental needs of his child. In this sense, the sensitive person can care about another's suffering even though he does not endorse the expressed wants of another.

One of the salient differences between sympathy and sensitivity is that the sympathetic person does not typically maintain a critical distance from the suffering of the other, whereas the sensitive person does typically maintain that critical distance. This difference is partially due to the fact that sensitivity involves a judgment about the moral legitimacy or worth of the wants or needs of others (or their long-run moral importance), whereas sympathy does not. Sensitivity involves an appraisal of another's wants and needs that is often made on moral grounds quite independent of the expressed wants of others.

Finally, sensitivity is the kind of attitude that provides strong *motivation*. The sensitive person is moved to act so as to minimize the harms and offenses that might otherwise result from his or her conduct. Attitudes in general have strong conative characteristics, and sensitivity (as well as insensitivity) is no exception. It is relatively uncontroversial, I believe, that sensitivity and insensitivity are attitudes that strongly motivate. But what is controversial is my view that this motivation is to some extent under the control of people who are insensitive, a state of affairs which matters for the ascription of responsibility. But before turning to that subject (in section 3), I will consider more closely (in section 2) the value of being sensitive.

2. Sense and Sensitivity

Various experiences have the effect of "desensitizing" people in terms of what I identified as the "caring" component of sensitivity. For example, a war veteran might become desensitized to killing and brutality because of continual wartime exposure to hideous atrocities. Sometimes being desensitized is like having a disease that has destroyed peripheral vision. Just as a partially blind person no longer sees certain objects, so an insensitive person no longer seems even to be aware of the harmful or offensive effects of his or her actions.

Some moral theorists conceive of certain features of moral judgment on the model of physical perception.[4] A person has the ability to discern from experience the moral facts, just as a person has the ability through the use of his or her eyes to discern physical facts. Moral discernment is not thought to be a rational intuiting of objective rightness or wrongness by some mental faculty. Rather, there is a subjective feeling of rightness or wrongness, which is said to parallel the feeling of pain experienced when, for example, a person grasps a hot poker. This pain is a contingent fact, for it may be that there are people who lack sensory feeling in their hands (either from birth or from some extreme accident). But most people are so constituted that when their hands are exposed to hot pokers, they feel pain. Similarly, it is thought that most people are so constituted that when they experience the suffering of others, they feel some kind of moral pain.

Although this concept of moral perception mistakenly blurs the distinction between sympathy and sensitivity, nevertheless it is a useful notion in several key respects. Sensitivity, as I use this term, shares with moral perception the key role of perceptiveness in moral judgment. One needs to be highly aware of the conditions of others, especially of the effect of one's own behavior on their well-being. Perceptiveness alone, though, will not account for the critical appreciation of which of those effects are beneficial and which are harmful. I am using the term "perceptiveness" in a way that does not make it a success word. A person may be aware of the world and yet not correctly appreciate the values of the things in that world. Correctly assessing the features of one's world involves a trait different from perceptiveness, namely, what I have been calling "critical appreciation." Perceptiveness alone will also not account for the ability to assess all morally relevant facts in order to reach a judgment of what ought to be done. Many theorists did not see that other features besides perceptiveness were necessary for explicating the judgment of morally appropriate action.

Sensitivity is best seen as a kind of meta-virtue, in that if one lacks sensitivity one lacks the kind of awareness and critical appreciation of the needs and feelings of others necessary to exercise appropriately one's other virtues.[5] Sensitivity involves appropriateness of response to the needs and feelings of others precisely because sensitivity is the virtue that requires that we carefully notice and care about the effects that our responses will have on other persons. Sensitivity supplies an essential ingredient for the proper functioning of at least some of the other virtues. In most cases, the nonvirtuous person fails because of some lack of perceptiveness or failure to appreciate the moral significance of the facts perceived. And in these cases, good intentions don't help much; indeed, good intentions combined with insensitivity often make things worse.

Consider a man who tries to be kind and generous to his son. He has recently learned that his son has overextended his credit. Even though the son has not asked for help, the man sends him a sum of money equal to his current debt. So far it appears that this is a virtuous act, especially since the intent is so clearly to express the father's love. But now imagine that the son is struggling for independence and has in the past displayed resentment of his father's similar acts. The son has been driven further and further away from his father due to these acts, which the son regards as his father's "interference" into his life. If the father is insensitive to the needs and feelings of his son, his good intentions will make it more likely that he will interfere, rather than less likely.

On this understanding, a sensitive person is aware not only of the way that his or her behavior will affect another, but also of other relevant facts of the situation at hand, such as whether someone is too easily offended or perhaps whether someone acts offended merely as a smokescreen when he simply dislikes what another person says. An appreciation of these facts is often necessary in order to determine which of several alternative actions is the most morally appropriate. Such considerations may lead to a decision not to do what was previously thought to be the virtuous thing. In this way, sensitivity sometimes acts as a corrective for the other virtues. The person who is insensitive but who has other virtues is likely to act in harmful ways due to a blindness to the facts. It will often not be possible for such a person to compensate for the lack of sensitivity in the same way that one might compensate for the lack of another virtue. For without sensitivity, a greater display of another virtue will not necessarily decrease the risk of producing harm to others. In the example of the generous father, things will not get better if the father becomes even more generous but remains insensitive.

The awareness that characterizes sensitivity is indispensable for making good judgments about morally appropriate behavior, just as perceptual awareness is indispensable for making good judgments about what to do in the empirical realm. The moral-sense theorists were right in pointing out that a certain kind of awareness is necessary for being moral. This is true with respect to judgments concerning appropriate behavior at the moment and also judgments concerning appropriate character traits in the long term. The formation and adjustment of character traits is dependent on the ability to form habits, and this ability is intimately connected to sensitivity. Just as the formation and change of our habits of attentiveness and understanding of visual details are based on a high level of sensory awareness, so the formation and change of our habits of good character are based on a high level of moral sensitivity.

A person who develops the habit of being insensitive will find it quite difficult to change his or her behavior even after recognizing that such change is morally valuable or required. One needs to be aware of how one's actions affect others, and also to appreciate the *moral* harm that can result, in order to see the need to change a particular attitude. In addition, as I will indicate in more detail later, one needs to be able to appreciate other people as like oneself in order to be able to see that they are deserving of the kind of behavior (for instance, benevolence or nonmalevolence) that one easily sees oneself as deserving. If a white male has an insensitivity to the plight of Blacks, for instance, then he will not recognize that they deserve respect; even when he eventually reaches this recognition, the habit of insensitivity may make it quite difficult for him to change his patterns of behavior.

In the next two sections I will consider a person's responsibility for being insensitive. The easy cases involve insensitivity that a person has chosen or is at least aware of and can now easily change. The hard cases involve a lack of awareness of, or extreme difficulty in changing, insensitive responses, perhaps due to the influence of stereotypic beliefs and attitudes. The harder the case, the more difficult it becomes to address in terms of a view of responsibility linked to what can be changed at the moment.

3. Insensitivity and Culpable Ignorance

Before turning to more difficult cases, I will provide an analysis of the moral responsibility for insensitivity in some of the easier cases. Let us begin by considering an extended analogy, namely, the case of a person who has lost her peripheral vision. Suppose that one day she is operating a car and because of lack of peripheral vision fails to notice a dog running perpendicular to the path of the car. She strikes the dog and injures it severely. It might seem as though she is not responsible for being unable to see the dog; insofar as this is the major fact, she would not be responsible for injuring the dog either. Analogously, if insensitive people are not responsible for their lack of perceptiveness regarding the reactions of others, then they are not responsible for the harmful consequences resulting from this aspect of insensitivity. In what follows, I will suggest the most obvious sense in which people are sometimes responsible for their lack of sensitivity.

The person who lacks peripheral vision might well be responsible for her visual condition or its consequences, if the condition is something she is aware of and if there are ways to alter the condition or minimize its harmful effects. If the woman is aware that she lacks peripheral vision, then operating a car is something she should do with extreme caution, if at all. The knowledge on her part that she lacks peripheral vision, that this condition is likely to cause harm, and that she could correct the problem are facts that override the fact that she was not responsible for losing her peripheral vision. The additional relevant facts make it *prima facie* appropriate to say that she is responsible either for her continuing lack of peripheral vision or for injuring the dog. A similar argument could be made about someone who becomes aware of his or her insensitivity.

I propose a general principle, which will form the focus of the rest of the chapter. This principle covers the cases considered so far, but will have to be amended later to cover cases of intractable insensitivity.

A person is responsible for a character trait (or its consequences) if either:

(a) the person was instrumental in developing the trait; or

(b) the person was aware of the trait and what could be done to change it (or minimize its harmful consequences), but did not try to change it (or to minimize its harmful consequences).

Most people seem to have the ability to influence somewhat their level of sensitivity. Consciousness raising, psychotherapy, and even making serious private resolutions can have an impact on how sensitive a person becomes or remains. If a person who can do so does not attempt to overcome insensitivity, then the person may be blameworthy because of moral negligence. Aristotle makes an analogous point quite well: "While no one blames those who are ugly by nature, we blame those who are so owing to want of exercise and care."[6]

Consider a second strategy. A person may be responsible for being ignorant in some particular way and for the effect of that ignorance on his or her behavior. The person may bear this responsibility, even if unaware of the harm he or she is likely to cause, in those cases in which the knowledge that was lacking was something that everyone in the person's position *should* have. For example, it is no defense against criticism of a president's administration for the president to plead ignorance of what high-ranking subordinates did in their official capacities; we believe that presidents *should not* be ignorant of such things. Ignorance is culpable if it violates well-accepted standards of what people in certain positions are expected to know.

Holly Smith argues that in one sense a person is not to blame for a culpably ignorant act because the motives that immediately gave rise to the act were not reprehensible. Indeed, she says that these motives may be innocuous or even praiseworthy. For example, a lifeguard who has negligently failed to learn a particular lifesaving technique calls the rescue squad to help save a victim whom the lifeguard cannot save because of ignorance about the required technique. But Smith also indicates a less obvious sense in which a person may be responsible even in such cases. The important consideration involves what she calls the "benighting act," that is, the act undertaken voluntarily in the past that now makes a current act not open to the agent.

One can be to blame for the occurrence of the risked upshot of one's act whether the upshot is an act or mere event. In cases of culpable ignorance, the unwitting act is a risked upshot of the benighting act, so the agent is to blame for it just as the [careless] hiker is to blame for [starting a forest] fire. . . [7]

In these cases, the responsibility arises by virtue of the benighting act and not from the motives existing at the present. The lifeguard should have learned the relevant technique in the past, since being a lifeguard carries with it the obligation to learn such things. It is no excuse in a crisis for the lifeguard to say that he cannot at the moment learn these techniques.

Analogously, in some cases of insensitivity people are responsible for their attitudes or beliefs because they *should* be cognitively aware of the likely effects of having various attitudes or beliefs. Of course, for it to be true that a person *should* be cognitively aware of such effects, it must be true that the person *could* be cognitively aware of them. Here we find an important difference between ignorance and insensitivity. The ignorant person often could have easily chosen to learn the morally important information. But it is not as easy to alter the nature of one's awareness at the moment as it is to seek out some needed information.

It should be pointed out that moral responsibility, indeed even blame, for ignorance is easiest to defend for those persons who would have found it relatively easy to be knowledgeable about harmful effects of their conduct that they did not in fact foresee.[8] In some cases of insensitivity, a person can rather easily become more sensitive simply by bringing the high attentiveness to detail characterizing other aspects of her or his life to bear on the needs and feelings of these persons with whom she or he interacts. Here, insensitivity can be handled completely on the model of culpable ignorance. For example, a father who is insensitive to the needs of his family members may be finely attuned to the needs of his prize tomato plants. Such a person could be faulted for not being as aware of the needs of his family as he has shown he can be toward his plants. But there are other cases of insensitivity that cannot be so easily assimilated to the model of culpable ignorance.

4. The Influence of Stereotypes

In some cases, the component of sensitivity at issue is critical appreciation, in addition to perceptiveness. If a person has stereotypic attitudes and beliefs, it is often not so easy to choose to be more sensitive, and it is not so obvious that the person is responsible ᵢₒᵢ his or her insensitivity. One of the chief difficulties with stereotypic and other intractable beliefs is that they block the attempt to understand the needs and feelings of individuals and of groups of individuals who are different from those holding the stereotypic beliefs or different from those who are currently esteemed. As a result, the critical appreciation of the suffering of others is made much more difficult than it would be otherwise.

"Stereotype" is defined as an "unvarying form or pattern, fixed or conventional expression, notion, character, mental pattern, etc., having no individuality, as though cast from a mold."[9] Stereotypes can concern members of human groups identified, for example, by race, sex, nationality, occupation, or sexual preference. These identifying features are regarded by people with stereotypic beliefs as invariant throughout a group's population. A stereotype is a kind of generalization that treats human groups as conforming to a pattern or mold. But in contrast to proper generalizations, a stereotype is resistant to counterevidence. Stereotypes are perpetrated by means of highly emotional language and images, which are so extreme as to break down possible communities that might be formed between those who hold the beliefs and those who are so characterized. The language of stereotypes is designed to demark social groups as completely distinct from one another. Of course, it masks the social reality that individuals are much more like each other than they are different.

Consider an employer who promotes male employees but not female employees, even when the female employees deserve to be promoted. When the female employees have performed in a meritorious fashion, he compliments this physical appearance and their determination, but he does not think of promoting them. He believes that men would be harmed if they were not rewarded with promotions for meritorious service, perhaps because he recognizes this need in himself. He sees that his female employees are being adversely affected by his actions, and in this sense he displays some perceptiveness. But based on his stereotypic attitudes toward women, he believes that his female employees are not hurt in any significant way by failing to advance their careers but are significantly hurt only when their femininity is adversely affected. The employer displays a lack of what I have been calling "critical appreciation" of the needs or wants of those who are affected by his actions. The difficulty is that someone who is behaving on the basis of stereotypic attitudes and beliefs often does not interpret his or her acts as producing suffering, even when they do. The stereotype may block the critical appreciation necessary to see someone's suffering as legitimate, or even as suffering at all.

Such examples seem to be at odds with analyses such as Iris Murdoch's, that claim that simply attending to another's suffering makes most people take that suffering seriously. Murdoch has claimed that the "more the separateness and differentness of other people is realized, and the fact seen that another man has needs and wishes as demanding as one's own, the harder it becomes to treat a person as a thing." But a person must be able to interpret another's suffering as actual human suffering first, and this involves more than merely perceiving that suffering. Murdoch admits some of this difficulty: "Goodness is connected with knowledge . . . which is the result not simply of opening one's eyes but of a certainly perfectly familiar kind of moral discipline."[10] Yet while the moral discipline involved in correctly appreciating what one is perceiving is "familiar," it is not easily attainable for those who have stereotypic attitudes and beliefs.

Even if one's insensitivity is the result of stereotypes, which cognitively block appreciation of the suffering of the stereotyped people, there may still be a sense in which one is responsible for that insensitivity. Following a distinction adapted from Harry Frankfurt, one might claim (although I would not) that a person is responsible for having a certain first-order attitude (a sexist attitude, in the example above) when there is a second-order (self-reflective) endorsement of the first-order attitude.[11] I have been arguing that it is often not appropriate to say that a person is responsible for such first-order attitudes since they are often formed in ways that are beyond the control of the person. But our second-order endorsements seem to be a more appropriate locus of moral responsibility. Regardless of how our first-order attitudes (for example, the attitude of insensitivity) are formed, it seems to be up to us to endorse or reject these attitudes when we reflect upon them. According to this view, it then does not matter that we are unable to change our first-order attitudes; we may still be responsible for them if we have reflected upon them and we have come to endorse them.

Implicit in this argument is the idea that people are in control of their second-order desires, dispositions, and attitudes. For if a person is not free to endorse or reject a given first-order attitude, we seem to have no better reason for saying that this person is responsible for the second-order attitude than for the first-order attitude. Yet some of what Frankfurt says at the end of his essay "Freedom of the Will and the Concept of a Person" is at odds with this move. He writes, "It seems conceivable that it should be causally determined that a person is free to want what he wants to want."[12] If it is so determined, then it would seem that second-order attitudes fare no better in terms of moral responsibility than do first-order attitudes and dispositions.[13] Here again the concept of a stereotype will exemplify the difficulty with a Frankfurt-style analysis.

Some stereotypes seem to operate at the level of second-order attitudes. Consider a white male who believes that Blacks are of inferior intellectual ability compared to whites. He comes to believe that Blacks will not be harmed if he does not even consider hiring them for positions that require strong intellectual abilities (supposedly including such things as coaching professional sports teams). It may very well be that such first-order beliefs and attitudes are the product of stereotypes. Now imagine that the man reflects on these first-order beliefs and attitudes and wonders whether they are racist beliefs and attitudes. At the second order, he may decide to endorse his first-order beliefs and attitudes because he decides that these beliefs and attitudes are not racist, since only people who are unintelligent, unlike himself, hold racist beliefs and attitudes.

On first glance it may appear that our second-order beliefs and attitudes are more fully of the self, and thus a more appropriate locus of responsibility, than our first-order beliefs and attitudes. But even at the level of reflection and endorsement of one's beliefs and attitudes, one's decisions may themselves be based on stereotypes and not under one's control. The racist beliefs in the example above may themselves be reflectively supported by stereotypes about intelligence. Hence, one's endorsements may not be any more under one's control than are the beliefs and attitudes one endorses. It is rarely the case that a person who holds stereotypic attitudes has contributed to the formation or even the subsequent endorsement of these attitudes. And also, it is often difficult for such attitudes to be overcome at a given time. Thus, in the hard cases I have been considering, there still may be so little control at the moment over a person's insensitive attitudes that it would be inappropriate to say that the person is responsible for the conduct that results from them.

5. Habits and One's Future Self

There is one more strategy that may help us decide whether people can be responsible for the sort of insensitivity that results from stereotypes about the natures or needs of others. Consider a person's habits, such as the tendency to associate with only certain kinds of people or the tendency to read only certain kinds of literature. Such habits may make it much less likely that one can easily overcome stereotypes. But if one's ability to change these habits is sufficiently under control in the long run, then one may be responsible for not changing the habits and perhaps also for the behavior that the stereotypes lead one toward.[14]

A part of responsibility for self is responsibility for one's habits, especially those habits that could cut off the possibility of change. Those who have stereotyped beliefs and attitudes may be currently unable to change. Once they become aware of these stereotypes, at least they are responsible for not reinforcing habits that would make it increasingly unlikely that changes in the self could occur in the future. Studies have shown that those who associate with people of different races are less likely to hold racially stereotypic attitudes.[15] If a person develops the habit of not mixing with people from other races, such a choice may curtail or impede the possibility of affecting stereotype-based insensitivity in the future. A person may become responsible for even intractable attitudes if he or she does not keep open the possibility for future change.

A habit is a disposition to act in a characteristic way in response to a given stimulus. Habits are formed over time, not at the moment, and hence planning and repetition are often required to form or change them. It is possible to form habits without realizing it, and it is often quite difficult to change the habits one has fallen into once one becomes aware of them. This is one reason why sensitivity is so important in the ability to control one's future self. A person who is not highly aware of the nature and effects of his or her conduct may fall into habits that will make it hard to become sensitive in the future and will make the conscious long-term control of his or her life very difficult.

A white person who has formed the habit of insensitivity to Blacks due to long association with people who are racists may never have consciously chosen to become a racist; for this reason he may not now be responsible for his racism. But he may be responsible for his racism in the future if he does not initiate steps now to change the habit of insensitivity. He will be responsible now if he decides not to initiate the steps necessary to plan for future change. The most obvious case of current culpability would involve someone who comes to understand his own racism and yet decides to increase his isolation from Blacks and to increase the amount of literature he reads that is racist in orientation. Such decisions will further entrench his racism and thereby increase his responsibility for the behavior which follows from his racist attitudes. But since racism is also due to social factors, no one person is *fully* responsible for the harms of racism.

Insensitivity provides an unusually clear example to consider concerning responsibility for habits. Since insensitivity includes the lack of awareness and critical appreciation of the needs and feelings of others, the more insensitive a person is, the less likely a person is to see correctly his or her place in a community of others. People who have the habit of insensitivity are so unresponsive to their environments that they are not aware of obvious facts about themselves, such as the harms that they are producing or at least risking. Among other things, insensitivity makes the conscience less able to operate, since one's own causing of actual suffering to others is not appreciated or even perceived. The conscience may thus be unmoved, even in someone whose conscience is mature. As I argued above, this is how insensitivity may block the proper functioning of other virtues.

Sartre provides an interesting analysis of attitudes that seem resistant to change. In *The Emotions,* he considers the case of a woman who has a phobia she seems unable to rid herself of. He writes: "The behavior of the subject is in itself what it is . . . but it is possible to decipher it by appropriate techniques as a written language is deciphered. . . . A consciousness which has not acquired the necessary technical knowledge would be unable to perceive these traces as *signs*."[16] Sartre proposes that psychoanalysis often provides the techniques to allow a person, over time, to understand attitudes or behavior that previously defied understanding. And such understanding is a significant step in the path toward being able to change.

Existential psychoanalysis, as well as other more empirically oriented versions of psychoanalysis and psychotherapy, can give a person control over some of the most deep-seated habits. Existential psychoanalysis reaches back to the "originary choices" that people make when they constitute themselves as distinct persons. The strategy is to begin with experience, that is, the "empirical behavior patterns," and then to attempt to reveal the underlying prereflective attitudes.[17] But it is rare that a person can perform this deciphering on his or her own. Rather, it is through a structured form of conversation that someone schooled in psychoanalytic technique can aid a person to uncover those choices of attitude that now sit like "half-calcinated pieces of wood" blocking conscious awareness and change.[18] But a person who is not aware that there are such hidden attitudes, because of a habit of insensitivity, is less likely to seek such assistance.

Insensitivity must be vigilantly guarded against. And this is why insensitivity that is recognized but not counteracted is something for which a person is morally responsible in the present. It now becomes necessary to modify slightly the principle I set out at the beginning of section 3, by adding clause (c).

A person is responsible for a character trait (or its consequences) if either:

(a) the person was instrumental in developing the trait; or

(b) the person was aware of the trait and what could be done to change it (or minimize its harmful consequences), but did not try to change it (or to minimize its harmful consequences); or

(c) the person was aware of the trait and the habits that supported it, but did not, at the time, initiate a plan to change the habits in the future.

A person is responsible at the moment for even stereotypic insensitivity if he or she chose in the past not to be open to the possibility of changing these attitudes, or if actions taken in the present make a future change of attitude much less likely. Here is one clear case in which a person may be responsible for a part of himself that, at the moment, is impossible to change. It is also an example of how responsibility does not depend on the current ability to do otherwise. But this way of approaching responsibility does not completely disconnect responsibility from the choices a person makes. Rather it expands our understanding of choice to include choosing our attitudes and habits. This is especially important since sensitivity is a meta-virtue affecting so many of our other dispositions. In cases of insensitivity, when the ability even to be aware of the suffering of others is affected, it is important to regard oneself as responsible for the kind of person one is and will become.

PART TWO

Omission, Inaction, and Groups

—

Groups and Personal Value
Transformation

In this chapter I will set the stage for a discussion of shared responsibility for the consequences of omission and inactions. Individuals in groups often fail to do those things that can prevent harm to others. People often do not recognize themselves as morally responsible for harms that occur within, and could be prevented by, groups, even though they often see themselves as responsible for harms that they witness, and could prevent, individually. Group membership is thought to diffuse one's responsibilities. In the following chapters I will argue against the diffusion of responsibility in groups. I will begin by examining some of the ways that harm is made more likely due to the fact that the values of individual persons change as a result of group membership.

There are two chief ways that a group brings about changes in the values of its members. First, in some groups the organizational structures, that is, the decision-making apparatus, the hierarchical ordering, the procedures and policies, as well as the absence of procedures and policies, function to bring individuals into conformity with the goals and values of the group. Second, in some other groups the identifications individual members make with other group members, that is, the solidarity, camaraderie, commonality of interest, or alienation from what adversely affects the whole, breeds a conformity of values within the group. In the first section, I will elaborate on this analysis of personal-value transformation in groups. In the second section, I will provide an elaborate example of how value transformation occurs. The example involves medical settings, such as an emergency room, in which both forms of change occur. And in the final section, I will begin the task of addressing shared responsibility for omissions, especially in organized groups. Throughout this discussion my goal is to show how an individual's values become intertwined with the values of groups the individual belongs to. A group's or a person's lack of action should be treated differently after the changes have taken place than it would have been before.[1]

1. Personal and Group Values

Individualism and collectivism are two common, and opposed, views about the relationships between individual and group values. Individualists generally claim that values are things that each of us decides about, or at least can decide about, quite independently of the groups or circumstances in which we happen to find ourselves.[2] Medical ethics literature is heavily influenced by individualism. This orientation at least partially explains why the moral dilemmas in medical ethics are almost always portrayed as problems for *individual* health care professionals. Should a physician administer lethal injections to terminally ill patients who want to end their lives? Should a nurse attempt to countermand an intern's orders if following the orders will run contrary to the expressed desires of the patient? Should a health care worker ever refuse to treat a patient who has a transmittable disease such as AIDS?[3]

I believe that individualism sometimes presents too simplistic a picture. People often come to act in ways they never would have otherwise chosen, as a result of the influence of groups. Many sociological studies confirm this, but most of us know it already just from reflecting on our own lives.[4] People who serve in the military are very quickly socialized to behave in ways they would never have believed possible, and certainly in ways they would not have chosen on their own. Individuals change their values when they have families, when they become members of large organizations, and when they are swept up in crowds and mobs. At the very least, people often find it hard to hold values greatly divergent from those of their fellow community members. To the extent that extreme individualism seems to deny this factor, it is misleading.

In contrast to individualism, collectivism is the view that groups are themselves entities that act in the world and that groups act in more fundamental ways than individuals. Individuals are really only parts of groups. There are no truly personal values that are uniquely chosen by discrete individuals; all of our ideas and values are imposed on us by the social groups to which we belong.[5] I am as suspicious of this view as of individualism. It seems counterintuitive to think that people can never overcome the strong influence of their communities. Indeed, while great conformity to group norms does exist, each of us has encountered a substantial number of people who are able to resist the influence of their groups. Whistleblowers and men and women of conscience appear in all societies and cast doubt on the collectivist explanations of human value formation.

My own position incorporates elements of both individualism and collectivism. In my view, groups are merely collections of individuals related in various ways. But the relationships make a huge difference. People do act differently in groups than they would on their own, because of the influence of these relationships. But ultimately, values reside within individuals, not within some kind of superentity called a "group." It is not the case that an institution, for instance, actually shapes the values of its members, even though we often talk in a shorthand manner as if it did. Rather, it is individuals within groups, operating through the formal and informal relationships or structures of the group, who influence the values of their fellow members.[6] Let me turn to the specific mechanisms by which groups, understood as I have indicated, affect the values of their members.

I will use two widely dissimilar types of group, the corporation and the mob, to stand for different ends of a spectrum of groups. They will help us make sense of two ways groups achieve the coherence that allows for collective action as well as for conformity to group goals and values. The corporation provides a good example of the role of organizational structure in the shaping of values of group members. And the mob provides a good example of the role of social identification, especially solidarity, in the shaping of values of group members. Most other groups, such as health care institutions, are hybrid groups which rely on both organizational structure and social identification in value transformation.

The corporation's decision-making structure, an elaborate mechanism for relating individuals within a subgroup, transforms the intentions and judgments of individual members of the board of directors into corporate ideas and judgments. The corporate decisions shape the attitudes and behavior of all the members of the corporation. Specifically, the corporation effects such changes by procedures and policies specifying how group members are to behave in their work roles. In general, the charter and other articles of incorporation define what it means to be "acting within the scope of one's authority on the job." Those who fail to perform the tasks clearly specified by corporate policy and procedure risk loss of job, as do those who act on the job in ways clearly outside the scope of their authority. Loss of job, and the corresponding loss of income, are the chief mechanisms motivating individual members to conform to corporate directives. But these are not the only motivators. The desire for promotion and advancement is also an important motivator, as is the desire to be respected within the community constituted by the corporation.

After a corporate decision has been made, there are a host of ways in which it can be implemented. Procedures and codes of conduct explicitly tell members of a corporation how they should behave on the job. Procedures set the agenda in terms of what things are to be taken seriously while on the job. Since supervisors or department heads decide questions of salary, promotion, and even retention, the cues they provide concerning what is proper and improper within the institutional setting are quite important to the lower-ranking members in deciding on their work values. Group members often adjudicate conflicts between personal values and work values on the basis of what they perceive to be their superiors' values. And it often happens that the corporation's values become the employee's values.

Often what is left unsaid by the *absence* of a procedure is more effective at bringing about behavior change than what is explicitly stated in procedures. In some contexts, serious risks are run when specific sorts of procedures are absent in a corporate setting. When issues are left off an institution's agenda, over time the members of the institution come to regard these issues as not important in their own understanding of their jobs. They are not matters even to be thought about, and certainly not matters to be given serious consideration.

If an issue that is left off a corporation's agenda is something that the institution's members really should be considering in their jobs, then the corporation's silence on the matter opens the possibility that its members may be encouraged to omit doing something to eliminate the risk of harm. For example, on university campuses, the absence of procedures and sanctions dealing with the sexual harassment of students by professors contributed for many years to an acceptance of this practice, or at least to an absence of concern for the problem, and hence to a greater tolerance of this practice than the members of the university communities might otherwise have had.[7] Similarly, the absence of procedures forbidding discriminatory treatment of patients on the basis of sexual preference contributed to harm against some AIDS patients. The American Medical Association has changed its policy and now urges that explicit procedures be adopted to protect AIDS patients.[8]

An even more pervasive influence that can transform personal values in corporations is the overarching policy that sets the goals for the whole corporate body. Role-defining or institution-defining policies often have a much stronger influence on a member's behavior than specific procedures. Their influence is pervasive because they are perceived by corporate members to set a moral tone for all the work-based experiences of the members. Consider the case of a corporation in which the role of a clerk is defined by an overarching policy that subordinates should do whatever is demanded of them by their superiors. The moral tone of this job is clearly one of servility, and over time the clerk will more and more conform his or her values, at least while at work, to those of the person whose demands he or she is obligated to serve.[9]

Studies in organizational behavior indicate that the policies and organizational structure of an institution have a very powerful effect on the behavior of the members of the organization. One reason for this is that policies and organizational structure "affect access to and authorization of decision making."[10] In addition, there is a kind of corporate ethic that arises within institutions. Any explicit policy that sounds like a general principle of behavior can take on the status of moral principle in especially large structures where there is no single person who assumes moral leadership of the group of members.

Role-defining and institution-defining policies have a profound effect on the moral values of the members of those institutions, because even when the values instantiated in these policies are not themselves moral values they have a stature and structure similar to moral values. Moral values are action-guiding and compelling in that they provide initial (or *prima facie*) reasons for behaving a certain way, independent of context. For example, the moral principle prescribing truth-telling is supposed to provide us with initial reasons to tell the truth regardless of what we are faced with. Role-defining or institution-defining policies create values that are similarly action-guiding and compelling.

The value of maximizing profit can easily replace moral values, at least in a restricted realm such as a workplace, and can transform the values of individuals who would normally place other values, such as service, ahead of profitability. Indeed, institution-defining policies can even become the kind of value that one feels *conscientiously* bound to uphold over other values. Huckleberry Finn felt conscientiously bound to turn in his friend Jim, in order to be relieved of the guilt he felt for harboring a runaway salve. Huck's feelings were based on values deeply instilled in him by his society through its institution of slavery.[11]

At the other end of the spectrum of groups, where there is little if any organizational structure, social identification can also play an important role in value transformation. By participating in a mob, people are enabled to act in ways they would not be able to act, and would not choose to act, on their own. When people join groups they become associated with others in ways that structure their self-perceptions. Group members influence one another by a certain kind of socialization, often not fully recognized by the group members, in which the values of the group member tend to be reshaped so as to conform to the norms of the majority of the members of the group. Mob members influence each other in such a way that people are encouraged to act in pursuit of goals and in ways they would never have allowed themselves if they had been uninfluenced by fellow mob members.

In mobs, individuals come to hold values different from those they would have held if they were not members of the group. These transformations of personal values are made possible because the group affects the way its members identify themselves. An extreme example is the wearing of hoods or masks by group members to hide literally the identity of the group member from others; the member is allowed, in a sense, to hide from himself or herself. Such a practice enables people to change their moral perspectives in order to conform with the practices of the majority of the group. Groups as diverse as sports teams, fraternal lodges, and hospital staffs often require their members to adopt a form of dress that makes them immediately recognizable as members of the group and that affects the way the members understand who they are.

One of the chief problems here is that the member of the group may identify so much with the group that his or her original moral values and sensibilities may be lost altogether. In lynch mobs, for example, some individuals completely lose their normal moral scruples, and their value priorities become inverted. One way that the lost moral scruples of the lynch mob member can be regained is through some kind of rehumanizing event. This process is well illustrated in the novel *To Kill a Mockingbird*.[12] A little girl asks hooded mob members about their children, who are her classmates. Her questioning breaks through their anonymity and makes it difficult for them to ignore their normal scruples.

It seems relatively uncontroversial to say that group membership often does affect an individual's values. What is not well understood is how radical transformation occurs. My hypothesis is that radical transformation occurs due to a combination of social identification and role-defining policies or practices.[13] Elements of both formal organization and social identification manifest themselves in many different institutional settings. Some role-defining policies will intensify and reinforce what individuals already feel in interacting with other members of the group. Values will be transformed more swiftly and certainly in such a setting. Let us next turn to an elaborate example of the kind of value transformation I have just sketched.

2. Risking Harm and Institutional Desensitization

Medicine and other health-related fields are often viewed as requiring special norms, quite different from the moral norms that are generally instilled in a person's conscience in a particular society. In most societies there is a close identification between causing pain to others and causing disharmony of the self.[14] People develop strong scruples against causing pain and actually come to feel something akin to pain if they cause pain to others. But in certain fields, like surgery, it is an impediment to efficiency to feel guilty every time one makes another person feel pain. It is a corollary of this view that health-related institutions *should* transform personal values, so that, for example, surgeons have diminished scruples about causing pain. Value transformation is possible because the perspectives and values of individuals can, at least temporarily, be transformed by the institution in which they work and with which they identify themselves.

When people are confronted by someone who is suffering greatly, their normal reaction is to display compassion, to feel suffering for the one who is suffering ("compassion" literally means "to suffer with" the one who is suffering). This is so to such an extent that many people become incapacitated because of their feelings of suffering at the sight of extreme suffering in others. But these normal feelings, so it would seem, must be changed in individuals who would be successful health care professionals. Indeed, medical institutions are often very efficient at transforming normal feelings and values, and the justification is rather straightforward: the coldly clinical approach is thought to be essential in performing the tasks associated with good health care. One textbook on emergency nursing warns, "If you are sympathetic and share the emotion with the patient, you lose therapeutic effectiveness: you may become unable to help the patient."[15]

In emergency rooms, individuals who are doctors, nurses, and even clerks are quickly socialized to behave quite differently than they would if they were anywhere else. The sight of intense human suffering often does not elicit revulsion, compassion, or even caring. Rather, the individuals who work in an ER simply become hyperefficient at the sight of horrors like crushed limbs. Only rarely do they react in the way they would if they confronted the very same scene on the way home from work. Sometimes the health professional's veneer cracks. The professional callousness may be destroyed by something deeply personal, such as recognizing the little boy on the ambulance stretcher as one's next door neighbor. But short of such occurrences, a professional veneer protects members of an ER staff from their all-too-human emotions. There is great utility in the fact that these individuals can remain cool and rational in the face of human tragedy, since the physical appearance or extreme suffering of those most in need of immediate treatment might, at least temporarily, incapacitate a person of normal sensibilities.

In the ER example, individuals are socialized to repress their normal compassionate reactions to those who are suffering. The feelings and values of the member of an ER team are, at least during working hours, quite different from what they would be otherwise. And what is often key is the harsh line drawn between working hours and nonworking hours. In my four years of working in an ER, I was struck by the unnatural tension that exists just below the surface, a constant foreboding reinforced by the sight of red phones (for ambulances to announce the arrival of heart attack victims and other emergency patients), police patrols, and warning signs on the walls, as well as by the intermingled sounds of sirens and gallows-style jokes late into the night. There is a solidarity among those who must catch a few minutes lunch break sandwiched between two equally unappetizing traffic accident cases. The carnage deadens one's moral sensitivity, and the camaraderie reinforces a coldly clinical attitude toward suffering and death. Indeed, the normal sympathetic reactions are often replaced by a callousness that would be utterly unacceptable in the "outside" world.[16]

This transformation of personal values takes place through what I have characterized as a combination of social identification and role-defining policies in an institution. A less extreme, although no less potent, example than the wearing of hoods in mobs involves the wearing of white coats or dresses (or green scrub suits) by the members of a health care team. The uniform acts to remind member and nonmember alike that the person wearing the uniform has a different set of moral priorities than those of nonmembers. The values and feelings of the group member are significantly affected by the other group members, and the uniform reinforces this changed perspective.

In addition, an Emergency Room is organized in such a way as to isolate the ER staff even from others in the hospital who are also involved in intensive care. The ER staff members are encouraged to become utterly immersed in their work; they often work long hours in close proximity to a few colleagues. Unlike mobs, Emergency Rooms do not contain unorganized individuals who are brought together by common interests. Rather, in the Emergency Room there is a decided organizational structure which contributes to the climate of social identification and aids in lowering the level of sensitivity of the ER staff.

As I mentioned above, it is undisputed that such a transformation of personal values serves an important social purpose. But significant risk is run whenever there is a radical change in the normal values and feelings of individuals in society. An army, for example, is able to accomplish its goals by diminishing the normal qualms its members have concerning harm to others; returning service men and women have difficulty stepping outside their now more violent personalities. These group members have sometimes caused harm or suffered psychological difficulties in civilian life because they have found it difficult to slip back into their normal roles once "outside" the group or institution.

There are problems that can occur "on the job" as well. A group of gung-ho soldiers might engage in a massacre.[17] ER personnel might find that their acquired insensitivity hampers their ability to diagnose properly certain subtle problems that are as much social as medical. For example, physicians may fail to put themselves in the shoes of attempted suicides. Desensitization to the sight of suffering may make it more difficult to respond appropriately to those who are suffering. There may be a failure to be attentive enough to the patient's own account of his or her suffering. Richard Zaner has detailed what is necessary for providing good health care: "A vital component of actual clinical thinking is appreciation of what the patient is going through, what things feel like to be the patient, including what is experienced, and its significance for him or her, without in any way taking advantage of one who is already disadvantaged."[18] The general worry here is that when normal scruples and sentiments are changed, there may be ancillary problems of desensitization, which may offset whatever good effects derive from medical socialization.

People in groups often do not act in the same way that they act as discrete individuals. This fact is causally responsible for both good and bad effects. On the positive side, people are often spurred on to greater than normal feats because of the inspiration, competition, or solidarity of finding themselves among many others who are all performing similar actions or working together for a common purpose. The members of a group often come to take on the values of the majority, submerging their own individual values into a group ethic, so as to be able sometimes to act conscientiously in ways that they could not allow themselves to act outside of the group. For example, surgeons are enabled to perform actions that people in normal circumstances would not be able to perform.

On the negative side, the transformation of values that often occurs when a person becomes a member of a group can be causally responsible for a great deal of harm. The overriding of personal values can sometimes thwart the operation of conscience altogether or invert the norms of the conscience so that people come to believe that the harm they are doing is morally right. In the former case, people are left morally at sea and ripe for exploitation by whatever may be able temporarily to substitute for morality, such as callousness or short-term profitability. In the latter case, members of a group may come to think of something as morally right that they had previously seen as morally repugnant outside of the group; a lynch mob exemplifies this process.

As I have been arguing, there is often a significant risk of harm when the normal scruples and values of individuals are altered. The kind of change that occurs among Emergency Room personnel may be short-lived, lasting only as long as individuals remain on the job. But more subtle and long-lasting changes can also occur. The risks here include long-term negative changes in the attitudes of health care practitioners toward the goals of caring and compassion. These changes may include an alteration in the very conceptualization of the health care professions themselves. Conscientious health care professionals may find themselves with inverted value rankings. They may feel "guilty" for spending too much time caring for patients who are unlikely to survive. ER personnel may find themselves feeling guilty for taking compassionate interest in particular patients and may come to neglect to do those things that can alleviate their patients' suffering. Medical institutions may fail to provide environments in which the moral character of their members can develop. I will next explore some of the implications of the foregoing for the notion that people have increased moral responsibilities when they share membership in groups.

3. Responsibility and Omission in Groups

The concept of shared responsibility seems quite appropriate for cases involving value transformation within groups. Personal-value transformation in groups has two important moral consequences for the way that we understand responsibility for harms that occur within groups. First, in groups people affect one another's behavior much more clearly than they do outside of groups. Since the members of the group influence one another to transform their values, there is a sense in which all group members share in the attitudes and behavior of all other group members. When a person is faced with the harmful actions of a fellow group member, that person's omission does not have the same status it would have if he or she were not connected to the harm-producing individual. When an individual's omission to prevent harm occurs within a group, the individual is likely already to be a partial contributor to the situation in which harm occurs. Second, individuals in groups are often socialized to be less sensitive to certain kinds of harm than they would be otherwise. As we saw in the case of the Emergency Room staff, people in groups sometimes experience the kind of value transformation that impedes the normal functioning of sensitivity. As a result, it is important for people in groups to feel a heightened sense of responsibility toward potential harms and hence to share responsibility for these harms, as a way of offsetting the possibility that group interaction will diminish the normal processes which operate to minimize harm.

Guilt is generally associated with some aspect of mind. In ethical theory it is the conscience that is the focus of feelings of guilt. In legal theory, a guilty mind (*mens rea*) or intent is often said to be a necessary condition of criminal liability. For individuals, guilt is normally considered to be tied to the mind in ways that require some kind of conscious, thinking self. Secondly, guilt has also been associated with a failure to do that which is expected and required in certain situations. The common term for this type of guilt is negligence. Here the mental component of guilt is diminished although not eliminated. Thirdly, there is a concept of shared guilt, which is connected more to who a person is than to the state of mind a person has.[19] Each of these three types of guilt—intentional guilt, negligence, and shared guilt—has a counterpart in group settings.

If we focus our attention on intentional guilt we will make little progress in changing conceptions of responsibility in groups. For those groups that are very tightly knit or have a decision-making structure, it may be that the institution acts and even takes on attitudes as a unit by exercising its equivalent of a mind. Such a situation was alleged to exist at Bob Jones University, where Blacks were discriminated against as a matter of university policy. In such rare cases, it seems appropriate to speak of collective intentional guilt for harm. But even in the Bob Jones case, there is not the same kind of intentional guilt that is displayed by individual persons, since the university's "mind" was at best conflicted, with a sizable minority of the community opposing its racist policies.

Unlike intentional guilt, negligence is often relevant in explaining the increased responsibility that a group's members should feel for harms that occur within the group. Since negligence concerns what people have failed to do, rather than what they have explicitly decided to do, negligence is applicable to groups as well as to individuals. To decide that a group of persons failed to act as it should have, it is not first necessary to answer thorny metaphysical questions about how it was that the group decided on its course. All that need be established is that the group should have taken certain actions, that it could have done so, and that it failed to conform to its duty. People in a group should feel negligent if they do not prevent harmful feelings, behavior, and attitudes from developing unchecked.

To set the stage for the discussion of negligence in the next chapter, let us return for a moment to the example of the emergency room. It is especially striking that desensitized feelings should flourish in hospital settings. Hospitals are supposed to be centers of curing and pain diminishment. Indeed, it seems clear to me that the members of a medical institution have a special obligation to confront potentially harmful practices which concern that for which they have been entrusted to provide care. It is quite clear that the members of a medical community may be negligent in not acting to counter the development of desensitizing feelings and attitudes among staff members when ancillary harms may result. It is no excuse from guilt merely to say that one does not hold the attitudes that are prevalent in one's community. The desensitized attitudes that are prevalent in medical institutions are properly a subject of guilt based on neglect by all members of these communities, given the nature of the institutions we have considered.

Responsibility in groups should be shared, especially when there are institution-defining policies that leave the door open for significant neglect of the humane goals of an institution. In medical settings, there are three overlapping types of negligence that are important in determining shares of responsibility for harms. First, there is negligence relating to the professional responsibility of each member of the medical staff. Second, there is negligence concerning what is left undone by the medical staff acting as a group. Third, there is negligence concerning the various policies and practices of the institution itself. In the next two chapters I will examine the general subjects of professional negligence and collective inaction to begin to see why members of groups often fail to do those things they could and should do toward the prevention of harm in the world.

Groups can be collectively responsible for various harms if the decisions, policies, and practices attributable to the group are themselves relevantly connected to those harms. But this does not yet answer the question of who should have the greatest share of responsibility within the group. It is often fairer to look to the leaders of a group, rather than to those members who merely allow others to engage in harm. The leading members are those who normally have the most direct input into the decisions of the group, and hence are those who most clearly share in whatever intentional decisions produce the harm. Most other members of groups have so little influence on group decisions that their own share in their institution's guilt is normally quite small (except in those few cases where they are the direct perpetrators or beneficiaries of the harmful practices).[20]

Failing to prevent another person from doing harm takes on

added moral significance when that person is a fellow member of a group in which value transformation has occurred. An individual's inaction or omission takes on a different cast when there are changes in attitude or behavior of others toward which the individual, along with others in the group, contributed. At the very least, such individuals should feel some sense of shared responsibility for the changes in value and perspective that have increased the likelihood of harm. I turn next to a discussion of negligence, especially professional negligence, to illustrate this point in greater detail.

FIVE

Negligence and Professional Responsibility

Negative responsibility concerns what a person fails to do, as opposed to what that person does. Examples include failing to prevent a fellow group member from causing harm or inadvertently allowing others to do harm. In this chapter I am especially interested in those failures of group members to act that are called acts of negligence. The view that a person is negatively responsible for harms in the same way that a person is positively responsible for harms has been attacked for diluting or diminishing personal responsibility in the moral and legal domains. In morality, negative responsibility is thought to encourage a person to put insufficient weight on responsibility for his or her own projects, as opposed to the projects of others that the person could prevent, and thereby to jeopardize the person's sense of moral integrity. In criminal law, negative responsibility is thought to encourage a person to put insufficient weight on responsibility for what she or he intends to accomplish, as opposed to what she or he has inadvertently done, and thereby to lose a sense of personal guilt. In both cases, shifting our concern from what a person intended to do and did, to what a person could have prevented others from doing, is said to disrupt the notion of personal blameworthiness and thereby to weaken both morality and the criminal law.

I will respond to this challenge by defending the notion of negative responsibility in the context of groups as an appropriate and important concept in morality and law. In the first section, I will set out a conception of negligence, explaining its relation to negative responsibility generally and distinguishing it from other conceptions that are more prone to criticism. In the second section, I will respond to an argument from moral philosophy by showing that employing a standard of negligence does not necessarily involve a loss of personal integrity. In the third section, I will respond to criticisms advanced in criminal law by showing that employing a standard of negligence does not necessarily involve a loss of personal guilt. At the end, I will explore the concept of professional negligence and indicate some of the dangers that result when negligence is left out of the conception of responsibility, especially in the context of a person's professional life. Throughout, I will attempt to render plausible this expansion of the normal understanding of responsibility.

1. Negligence and Due Care

Surely the central difficulty with the notion that a person is responsible for what he or she has failed to do is that there are so many things that one could have done that one's potential failures seem to be endless. A theory of negligence attempts, among other things, to provide a guide for determining which of one's omissions should be clearly subject to moral or legal blame and guilt. It is not sufficient that a person failed to act in a way which would have prevented harm to others. In law, only certain omissions will be considered negligent, namely those which meet certain rules concerning avoidability and reasonableness. Prosser and Keeton, summarizing over a century of work in negligence theory, explain the rationale as follows:

> Such rules are adopted because the line must be drawn somewhere, and if the defendant is to be held liable merely because he has ridden the horse or driven the car, it would be quite as logical, at least in the eyes of the law, to hold the driver liable for owning it, or even for drawing his breath or being born. To hold that a person does every voluntary act at his peril, and must insure others against all of the consequences that may occur would, in most instances, be an intolerably heavy burden upon human activity.[1]

They also provide us with a good analysis of legal negligence. Negligence is a kind of conduct that has four necessary, and jointly sufficient, conditions:

1. A duty or obligation, recognized by the law, requiring the person to conform to a certain standard of conduct, for the protection of others against unreasonable risks.
2. A failure on the person's part to conform to the standard required: a breach of the duty. . . .

3. A reasonably close causal connection between the conduct and the resulting injury. . . .
4. Actual loss or damage resulting to the interests of another. . . . The threat of future harm, not yet realized, is not enough.[2]

In law, negligence is treated as a kind of risky behavior resulting in harm to others. But not all risky behavior resulting in harm is legally actionable. Rather, legal blame will be assigned only to risky behavior that violates a recognized legal duty.

In Anglo-American law the standard of conduct that people are generally obligated to follow is the standard of "due care." "Due care" is defined as what a reasonable person would suppose to be required in a given situation. This standard becomes clearer the more the features of a reasonable person can be specified. As one might expect, certain features of the reasonable person are more controversial than others, such as whether such a person should know what the likely long-term effects are of his or her actions. In morality, a reasonable-person standard is often proposed to identify which negligent omissions should be singled out as those for which one is especially responsible.[3]

When a person is a member of a group that publicly declares its members to have various competencies and skills, it is much easier to specify what "due care" means for this person than when he or she is merely someone on the street. A reasonable doctor, for instance, will be expected to know quite a bit about how to treat a given injury, whereas it is not true that a mere reasonable bystander will be expected to know how to treat medical injuries. It is often not clear whether a bystander should be expected to try to help an injured person, or whether, given the bystander's lack of medical knowledge, he or she should be expected *not* to try to help.

While the mere threat of future harm is generally not enough to satisfy the fourth condition of negligence (actual loss or damage), having various risk-taking attitudes sometimes violates the reasonable-person standard used in the first condition. Bystanders are expected to be cautious in their behavior toward others, especially when the others are already injured; the risk-taking bystander may indeed be regarded as someone who failed to exercise due care and hence as someone who acted negligently. Doctors are expected to be cautious, but they are also expected to have the kind of knowledge that would enable them to go to the aid of the injured.

It has sometimes been contended that the model of legal negligence cannot be readily adapted to the moral domain because there is no moral standard of due care in everyday life. Robert Merrihew Adams, for instance, asks the following question:

> Is there a standard (however imprecise) of due consideration of ethical issues to which we hold rational agents in general? Is it a sin to graduate from college without having taken a course in ethics (or two or three) if it would not have been an enormous personal burden to take one? I don't think so—much as the general acceptance of such a claim might improve the employment prospects of philosophers.[4]

Adams is surely right to think that "due care" is much harder to define in ethics than in law, but I don't think he is right to think that there is no conventional standard of due care in the everyday roles people assume. Lifeguards are viewed morally in much the same way they are viewed legally, that is, by reference to a standard of reasonableness. While this standard may vary somewhat over long periods of time, it is largely constant at any particular period, although it has little to do with what is commonly taught in ethics courses.

In the *Nicomachean Ethics,* Aristotle says that if a person injures another person "in ignorance" the errant act may be culpable if the injury happens "not contrary to reasonable expectation," that is, if it could have been reasonably expected. For an "error is culpable when the cause of one's ignorance lies in oneself."[5] People should take reasonable precautions against the infliction of injury on others. "Due care" is the moral requirement that a person in various roles act in ways in which any reasonable person would act. If a reasonable person would not leave the lifeguard platform to chat with a friend, then it is contrary to the due care requirement of moral negligence for a particular lifeguard to do so. The lifeguard could thus meet the due care condition for moral negligence even while claiming, correctly, to have been ignorant of the risks the conduct created for swimmers.

Moral negligence is most plausibly seen when there are obvious likely consequences of an act, such as the act of shooting a weapon into a crowded street. There are widely understood reasonable precautions for anyone who handles a dangerous weapon, since the risk of fatal injury is an overriding concern of any reasonable person.

The cases get harder when what is risked by the omission is less clearly of overriding concern. A person's failure to contribute to Ethiopian famine relief is not so easily determined to be a case of moral negligence. It may turn out that enough other people contribute to famine relief that one person's failure to contribute does not by itself result in deaths by starvation in Ethiopia. And in some cases it is reasonable to anticipate the actions of others and to predict that one's own failure to act will have no harmful effects. Due care requires that people in various roles take reasonable precautions against injury to others, but it does not require that people take precautions against any possible injury.

Standards of due care are easiest to apply when a person has undertaken well-defined roles, on the basis of which reasonableness can be ascertained. What it is reasonable to expect of a lone bystander is quite difficult to determine, short of saying that it is expected that each person should try to avoid injuring others. But if a person has voluntarily joined a group, for example a professional group such as doctors or engineers, then it is often relatively easy, in both law and morality, to ascertain what would count as negligent behavior on this person's part. Most professional groups are at least partially defined in terms of the public expectations associated with membership in the groups. Consider the example of the group of lifeguards. The group is defined by the public expectation that its members will, for instance, be prepared to jump into choppy waters to try to save a drowning person. Lifeguards are thus expected to perform various tasks, when faced with a drowning bather, that ordinary bystanders are normally not expected to perform. If a person who has voluntarily assumed the social role of lifeguard does not, for instance, attempt to swim out in choppy seas to save a distressed swimmer, he or she is considered to be *prima facie* negligent, whereas this would not be true of an ordinary bystander.

Group membership also provides another basis for negligence. As we saw in the previous chapter, when a person joins a group then the potential for harm, as well as the potential for good, is greatly increased. Collective action is a much more potent force in the world than individual action. When people join groups they greatly expand what they can accomplish in the world, but they also expand what they are responsible for. The members of groups share responsibility for many of the harmful practices of their groups. If a particular group member could have prevented a particular harm from being perpetrated by the group, then that member may be negligent for not preventing harm in ways not applicable to nongroup members.

Collective action is only possible in groups because all of the members either participate in or facilitate group action. Often facilitation means being in a position to block others from acting, but choosing not to block their action. As we will see later in this chapter, groups such as professions derive various benefits from society, and their members must be seen as having to pay corresponding costs for their increased ability to influence the world. For this reason, group membership creates a standard of care, in accordance with which members are expected to prevent fellow members from causing harm. When people voluntarily join groups, they thereby increase their moral and legal duties. Claims of negligence are thus more appropriately made against people in groups than against people acting alone, unconnected to others. Herbert Fingarette has taken this point and extended it to a larger section of the population:

> In accepting responsibility as a responsible *person* we tacitly engage ourselves to take on a vast, and antecedently unspecifiable, range of specific responsibilities. The responsible person is one who has learned to identify a reasonable variety of these when he comes upon them. And he distinguishes these cases where he is antecedently committed from those very many cases where he is antecedently uncommitted. He knows the ropes, although there is no rule book.[6]

Group membership involves the sharing of responsibility for certain harms by all or most of the members of the group. Those members who did not directly perpetrate the harm, but who nonetheless share responsibility for it, are most often implicated in the harm due to their negligence in not having taken steps to prevent the harm. In the next two sections of this chapter I will argue that expanding the domain of responsibility to include the type of negative responsibility that I have been calling "negligence" does not diminish the importance of the concept of positive responsibility that people already recognize. In the final section of this chapter, I will address in more detail the advantages of adopting a standard of negligence in the context of professional responsibility. This is surely the least controversial part of the project of expanding moral responsibility to include a concern for omissions and inaction, although it is not without its critics.

2. Integrity and Omissions

One way of understanding moral negligence is to think of the "neglect" in reference to what a person knows, in his or her conscience, to be right.[7] Another way of understanding moral negligence is to think of the "neglect" in reference to what a person failed to do to prevent harm. In the former case, one neglects to *think* about one's principles; in the latter case one neglects to *act* to prevent harm. In the present chapter and the next, I will be primarily concerned with the latter type of moral negligence. In this discussion, moral negligence will involve the failure to exercise due moral care, where exercising moral care is understood to involve the prevention of various types of harm that a person could have prevented.

It might be thought that the prevention-of-harm criterion of the duty of due care creates the following problem: that my own projects, which I would choose to engage in, are not given any higher priority than projects of others, which I could prevent but the prevention of which I would not choose if doing so conflicted with my own projects. As a result, negative responsibility seems to diminish my moral freedom to choose how to live my own life by simply deciding which projects of my own to pursue. Others can exert undue influence on how I choose to lead my life by adopting plans which call for me to drop everything so as not to fail to prevent them from pursuing their harmful plans. As Bernard Williams puts it:

> It is absurd to demand of such a man, when the sums come in from the utility network which the projects of others have in part determined, that he should just step aside from his own project and decision, and acknowledge the decision which utilitarian calculation requires. It is to alienate him in a real sense from his actions and the source of his action in his own conviction.[8]

If I, as a member of a group, expect that Jones, a fellow group member, will injure Smith and that I can prevent Jones from committing such injury, then it would, all other things being equal, be morally negligent of me not to prevent this injury. If there are enough people like Jones in the world, then I will have to spend all of my time preventing their injuries to the Smiths of the world, and I will always have to put the prevention of the projects of the Joneses ahead of the pursuit of my own projects. I will never be able to give priority to my own life plans and thus will be alienated from my own moral convictions.

It might be thought that the problem could be remedied by placing responsibility for our commissions (positive responsibility) ahead of responsibility for our omissions (negative responsibility). I wish to challenge this assumption. Consider the case of a doctor who believes that elderly cancer patients should not be told how little hope for recovery they really have; hence, she omits to disclose information to such patients. Assume that a particular elderly patient wishes to know all there is about his ailment (which turns out to be cancer). If commissions are put on a higher plane than omissions, the doctor will not feel less alienated from her own projects, since she will then be forced to disclose rather than to refrain from disclosing the information. Indeed, the omission of the disclosure is what the doctor's own convictions would favor. The problem is not with putting omissions on the same level as commissions, but rather with the fact that people feel obligated to do things that are contrary to what they would otherwise want to do. Sometimes the choices that confront a person are alienating because they are contrary to the person's plans, and sometimes they are alienating but not contrary to such plans. But it is wrong to think that giving priority to negative responsibilities over positive ones necessarily increases the alienation one feels.

There is no good reason to see omissions as less a part of one's life plans than commissions. The doctor may make it part of her life plans to omit disclosing information to patients, just as the doctor may make it part of her life plans to disclose such information. The assumption of the role of doctor carries both positive and negative responsibilities. The doctor may decide to refrain from disclosing information to a patient out of a professional conviction that such a disclosure is generally harmful to a certain type of patient, and this conviction may be more important to her than some of the things she has decided to do that require commissions. Alienation and loss of moral integrity do not seem to correlate directly with putting omissions and commissions on the same level.

But there is a serious problem with negative responsibility if there is no limit placed on the range of omissions a person can be blamed for. Our omissions are potentially infinite in number, and to worry about them all as much as we worry about our commissions would leave no time for anything else in our lives. But this objection does not confront those who defend the type of negative responsibility called "moral negligence." For moral negligence, as I have argued, is a way of restricting the range of blameworthy omissions. We do not have to worry about what every Jones is currently doing to every Smith. Rather, we are only morally required to pay attention to those actions of others that risk harm and that, given our roles, it is reasonable to think that we should try to prevent.

Moral integrity is not assaulted by a thesis which places high priority on the class of negative responsibilities called "morally negligent omissions." Only a very indiscriminate consequentialist, one who fails to distinguish among *types* of omissions, falls prey to this criticism. It is morally negligent to fail to do what someone in a similar role is reasonably expected to do. This reasonable-person standard is clearest in application in those cases in which a person has assumed an office with clearly defined role expectations. In other cases, there are at least a few rules of thumb, such as that harm is to be minimized.

In general, a person is expected to act in the way that a group of reasonable fellow community members would expect of that sort of person. This moral standard of the reasonable person obviously has much in common with the reasonable-person standard in law. The legal standard is often ascertained by reference to the decision of a committee of randomly selected community members, known as a jury. The jurors are asked to determine what was reasonably expected of the person charged with negligence. In the case of moral negligence, we should try to ascertain what our various roles have committed us to. To do this, one strategy would be to imagine a group of fellow citizens and to ask whether this group would feel that it is reasonable to expect us to prevent a certain harm. If the answer is "yes," then it would be morally negligent not to attempt to prevent the harm. Let us next turn to various legal theorists who object to placing negligent acts on a par with intentional acts in criminal law.

3. Personal Guilt and Negligence

A standard criticism of negligence in criminal law is that it breaks the normal link between personal conduct and criminality.[9] The *mens rea*, or guilty mind, requirement in law is thought to epitomize this linkage. Yet it is claimed that *mens rea* is not a requirement well suited to negligence, which is itself not really a state of mind at all. A. D. Woozley has well summarized this position.

> If negligence is to be called (partly) a state of mind, it is so in a very stretched and negative way: to be told that a per-

son was not attending to, thinking of, or noticing something that he should have been is to be given some information, of a negative sort, about his state of mind, but it tells us very little, for it eliminates only one of an unlimited range of states in mind (in the positive sense).[10]

Because negligence is not really a state of mind in the first place, it is difficult to claim that negligence involves a form of *mens rea*. Yet if negligence does not involve a type of mental guilt, then, others would claim, it should have no place in criminal law, since criminality would be weakened if it did not remain connected to some type of personal guilt.

I would readily admit that negligent acts are not on a par with intentional acts in terms of *mens rea*. But I wish to argue that the dispositions and attitudes involved in negligence retain enough at least semiconscious awareness that it is not inappropriate to say that negligent acts contain an element of *mens rea*. And this position would provide a response to the claim that employing negligence in criminal law encourages people to lose a sense of personal guilt. I will begin by responding to Woozley's point that negligence can only be called a state of mind in a stretched and negative sense.

At the beginning of this chapter, I followed a long line of legal and moral theorists in defining negligence as a form of behavior, not a state of mind. By this I did not mean to imply that negligence does not *involve* a state of mind. There is a category of attitude and disposition that is typically involved when someone acts negligently. Carelessness, thoughtlessness, and insensitivity are all attitudes that are usually involved in negligent behavior, in the sense that they are often responsible for a person's failure to act reasonably. And given that attitudes are states of mind, negligence usually involves states of mind, in the sense that negligent acts are caused by, or intimately involved with, various attitudes. These attitudes and dispositions are not merely "negative," in Woozley's sense, for they are more than descriptions of what is lacking in someone's state of mind. Even though they are all etymologically connected to a lack (e.g., care-*less*-ness), they stand for mental states in which the person has a con-attitude toward doing certain things in a given situation. A con-attitude is not merely an absence of a pro-attitude. Rather, it involves a disposition to behave a certain way that is conscious, or at least semiconscious. In this sense, negligence does involve a state of mind, even though not necessarily an intentional state. In previous chapters I indicated that there are important attitudes and dispositions of which we are enough aware to make them the proper subject of moral appraisal.

Defenders of the view I am opposing would say that our nonintentional states are so much less under our control than are our intentional states that the sense of being an agent may be lost if people come to feel personally guilty for what they have not intended to do. For this reason they contend that negligence should not be placed on the same level as intentional wrongdoing. But it seems to me that what is crucial to seeing oneself as an agent is recognition that it was truly *oneself* that made choices that played a causal role in a given harm, and that there were things one should have done differently so as to prevent that harm. Seeing oneself as an agent requires paying attention to more than simply one's intentional acts, although it does not require placing one's intentional acts on the same plane as one's nonintentional or semiconscious acts. I take up this issue in greater deal in the final chapter of this book.

Christine Sistare has a very interesting alternative way of understanding negligence and *mens rea*. In her book *Responsibility and Criminal Liability,* she argues:

> Negligence is a special instance of prior fault. The negligent agent is culpable not because of the immediate *mens rea* or condition with which she acts but because of her responsibility for "getting into" the pertinent condition. . . . The pretense that inattention or unawareness are mental states is difficult to support. Indeed, there is no principled way to distinguish unawareness establishing negligence and exculpatory unawareness without reference to the concept of prior fault which most cognitivists abjure.[11]

I find some of this argument quite appealing. Negligent inadvertence can indeed only be ascertained in the context of what the agent has already done. For example, if a person has promised to watch a beach area for swimmers in trouble, it is negligently careless of him to be distracted by a game show on his portable television set and as a result not to hear the screams of a drowning swimmer. Here carelessness is a condition for which we can only assign negligence in light of the other intentional acts taken previously by the "lifeguard". His "prior fault" has to do with the intentional act of turning the television set on too loud to hear a swimmer's screams; he chose to do something to obstruct his hearing. Carelessness, although perhaps not negligent carelessness, would also have occurred if the life-guard had simply been daydreaming (and as a result didn't hear the screams of the drowning swimmer).

While I thus concur in large part with Sistare's analysis of *mens rea* and negligence, I nonetheless believe that negligent carelessness does involve a mental state at the time of the harm. The television-watching lifeguard is responsible both because of his choice to watch television, when he should have been listening for swim-mers' screams, and because of his semiconscious mental awareness of what he was doing, namely, neglecting his chosen duties. But it is clear that this mental state is not an intentional mental state.

I agree with Woozley and others in thinking that it is a mistake to talk of negligence as involving the same type of *mens rea* as inten-tional wrongdoing. The kind of mental guilt involved in negligence, whether it is mere inadvertence or the more conscious states of carelessness and insensitivity, does not require the high degree of awareness that is involved in intentional wrongdoing. It is thus a mistake to treat the mental component of negligence in the same way as that of intentional wrongdoing. But a person's appreciation of the guiltiness of her or his attitudes, dispositions, and behavior is not adversely affected by grouping both mental states loosely as *mens rea* states, as long as people remain aware that what is blame-worthy is that their chosen dispositions, attitudes (conscious as well as semiconscious), and behavior *caused* harm that they should have prevented. As long as the link between personal agency and per-sonal guilt remains clear, the notion of blameworthiness that under-girds our notion of criminal guilt will not be adversely affected.

Shared agency is, as I argued in chapter 2, connected to the con-tributions that a person's chosen action or inaction makes to a partic-ular result. I will return to this issue in the final chapter. Suffice it here to say that what a person is negligently guilty of will still con-cern the effects of what he or she has chosen not to do. Reasonable-ness will be the guide in discovering whether an absence of action was of the sort that should be seen as negligent. By this method, there will still be a link between a person's mental states, that per-son's conduct, and the judgment of criminality.

4. Moral Integrity and Professional Negligence

So far I have argued that negligence does not fall prey to several common criticisms against standards of negative responsibility in morality and law.[12] I wish to conclude this chapter by providing two positive reasons for urging that people, especially members of various professions, feel responsible for their negligent acts. In fact, both reasons concern matters we have already explored. Having a concept of negligence normally helps people to lead lives more integrated with their other values; it also provides an easily applicable way to begin to distinguish appropriate from inappropriate feelings of guilt. The area of professional conduct reveals best how the concept of negligence accomplishes these two tasks. I will explain these points in more detail, but I wish first to make some conceptual comments about the nature of professional responsibility, as well as of moral integrity.

As with any standards of negligence, standards of professional negligence are based on reasonable expectations by the public concerning those who profess to do various kinds of work. Professional negligence involves the neglect of duties the professionals have assumed. These duties are finite in number and determinable by reference to the reasonable-person test I set out in the first section of this chapter. In the next chapter I will discuss the basis for some of these more general duties, especially the duty to prevent suffering. For the moment, though, I assume without argument that a finite list of duties for each profession is feasible, once we understand what a profession is.

Increasingly in our society, groups of individuals who share a common expertise and who desire to enhance their social status come to regard themselves as constituting a profession. In each case, the emerging profession struggles to identify its unique status in the larger society and often struggles to convince other organizations and institutions to grant it a certain amount of autonomy in decision making. To secure such a status, emerging professional groups (such as teachers) create codes of conduct, which serve to indicate to members the obligations and ideals of the profession, as well as to demonstrate to the public the profession's willingness to police its own members according to standards and sanctions promulgated by the group itself.

Black's Law Dictionary defines a profession: "The term originally contemplated only theology, law and medicine, but as applications of science and learning are extended to other departments of affairs, other professions also receive the name, which implies professed attainments in special knowledge as distinguished from mere skill."[13] For centuries, the "professed attainments in special knowledge" has propelled professionals into special classes in our society. Indeed, the earliest professional associations were guilds, which engaged in protective activities much like contemporary trade unions. Today, the individuals who profess special knowledge often form themselves into groups bound together by the common privileged status each member seeks. Membership criteria and internal codes of conduct are then adopted, as a public statement that each member wants to be recognized predominantly as a member of a privileged group. In this manner the individuals voluntarily enter into various organizational affiliations, which have the effect of allowing the individuals to describe their own actions as professional actions, that is, as the actions of members of a group that professes to have special knowledge. When the group takes upon itself the task of publicly judging the quality of services or products that fall within its professed area of expertise, it further promotes its public image as a group of which each member has knowledge allowing him or her to make judgments that members of the general public are not capable of making. It is in this way that the actions and judgments of individuals come to be linked with the special status of the professional group.

Once the identification is made between the status of the individual and the privileged status of the group, the individual is said to make professional judgments and actions. The group in effect licenses the descriptive transformation of the judgments and actions of the member. The licensing is sometimes quite literal and sometimes only tacit, but the effect is the same: the individual can describe his or her actions as the actions of a member of a profession. Thus, in becoming a member of a professional association an individual is publicly declared to be competent. Of course, it is also true that the actions of the individual, now seen as professional actions, rebound and affect the status of the group. Concern over this fact has led many professional groups to form themselves into professional associations with rules of conduct, which are enforced against each of its members. It is in this way that the group attempts to prevent diminution of its public image due to the unsavory conduct of one of its members.

With the establishment of associational rules of conduct for all of the members, an even tighter identification can be made between the individual and the group status. When one member of the association uses the expression "in my professional judgment," it is assumed by the public that he or she is speaking for the profession, or at least a sizable number of its members. All professional associations are structured in such a way that their members can be identified by the public. Thus, all professional associations have at least an informal ability to control their members, by publicly disassociating the group from the member in question. Since all of the members seek the benefits of identification with the professional association, censure and disassociation are serious clubs that the association can threaten to use against its wayward members.[14]

Professional responsibility means regarding oneself as personally accountable for the effects of one's professional judgments and actions. Often discussions of the professional responsibilities of distinct professions center on the micro-ethical level; the questions of honesty and fairness are surely the most important micro-ethical principles relevant for day-to-day dealings of professionals with other individuals. The professional tries to find the mean between serving society and serving his or her own interests. Professional negligence arises when a professional fails to do that which, as commonly recognized, any member of the profession should have done. Professional negligence is understood as limited by the roles a person has assumed; it can be quite narrowly defined.

Moral integrity involves, as Socrates characterized it so well, a state of being in harmony with oneself. A person tries to bring his or her behavior into line with his or her principles; this integrating of behavior and principles is what is called integrity. When one fails, one feels pangs of guilt for failing to live up to the standards one has decided to live up to. Moral integrity also involves a sense that one is able to decide which life plans are best for oneself and to give these plans extra weight, as compared with those life plans that others might have. But that moral integrity cannot be used to shield a person from the effects of his or her own attitudes and behavior on others. Moral integrity involves the notion that our own actions and omissions need to conform to our principles, for we are responsible for what we do and who we are. In short, the morally integrated person cannot avoid thinking in terms of negative as well as positive responsibility, at least not without extensive self-deception and alienation.

The morally integrated person cannot, as Adolph Eichmann did, simply ignore the effects of a part of his life, so that his principles do not confront those behaviors and attitudes that would fall below his own standards.[15] Eichmann claimed that his major life plan was to be a loyal soldier and bureaucrat. In order to achieve his goal,

Eichmann felt it was increasingly necessary to ignore the effects of his bureaucratic actions on Jews, Gypsies, and other undesirables. If he had *discovered* how many people he could have saved from extermination, he would have been conscientiously incapable of following the role of good soldier and bureaucrat he had set for himself. That these deaths were likely to occur did not result from any positive, intentional acts of his own. Would Eichmann's moral integrity have been violated if he had acted contrary to his life plan just so as to save the lives of people he had not himself put in jeopardy?[16]

Such an analysis shows the counterintuitive results of too narrow an approach to moral integrity. One can imagine Eichmann being in harmony with himself only by ignoring the world around him. And such a strategy seems indeed to be the one he actually employed. But then his life was harmonious only at the cost of gross self-deception, namely, his delusionary belief that Jews and Gypsies were not dying in large numbers at the hands of the people he supervised. It is also true, though, that even as Eichmann was to a certain extent thereby able to issue orders and hence to be a "good" bureaucrat, he failed himself in other respects. For it was not possible for him to be a "good" soldier or bureaucrat, at least in terms of being professionally vigilant about the activities of his subordinates, and to blind himself to the activities of those whom he had *agreed* to supervise. By failing to live up to the role expectations he had agreed to for his supervisory position, Eichmann went against his own commitments and thus violated his moral integrity. Someone who voluntarily assumes a professional role in a society, such as supervisor, should not, without good reason, fail to do what is normally expected concerning that role. For to do so would be at odds with what the same self had already agreed to do.[17]

It is in this way that Eichmann's life may be said not to be morally integrated. He scrupulously followed the orders given to him, never trying to investigate fully his supervisees' actions, the knowledge of which might have made it harder for him to follow his orders. And insofar as he did what his Nazi superiors expected of him, he was perhaps somewhat true to himself. But at the same time his negligent failure to find out what his supervisees were doing, and hence to discover the harm that he was facilitating, violated his own agreement to perform supervisory tasks. While being morally integrated in the sense that he was able to live with his conscientious convictions, he failed to be integrated in the sense that he did not do that which he had agreed to do. The failure to investigate fully what his supervisees were doing meant that he remained conscientiously un-affected by their acts. But such conscientiousness violated what he would conscientiously have felt if he had been made aware of the plight of those who were suffering at the hands of his supervisees. Moral integrity demands that he not act negligently; it means that he not do what, in full knowledge, he would not have conscientiously done. Of course, I here skirt the question of what is to be said to those people, apparently unlike Eichmann, who could "conscien-tiously" participate in mass murder.

Furthermore, employing a standard of negligence also has the ad-vantage of diminishing the potential for unreasonable personal guilt that people might feel when they become aware of suffering in the world. As I pointed out earlier, negligence standards in law provide a way to render manageable the vast number of things it is in a per-son's power to accomplish, but that the person has failed to accom-plish. A person is not legally negligent unless a judge or jury would find it reasonable to expect that a person occupying a similar role should perform the action that he or she failed to perform. Similarly, in morality a person should not feel morally guilty unless it is rea-sonable to think that a person in the same role and situation should have done what he or she failed to do. If it is not reasonable to think that a person should have performed a certain action, then it is not morally negligent for the person to have failed to do it. And this means that there is also no good reason for someone to feel person-ally guilty for this omission. In the next chapter I will consider cases in which a person's inaction may make him or her responsible in a way less accusatory than that which involves guilt. In this discus-sion, though, I will not claim that weaker forms of responsibility are on a par with forms of responsibility, such as negligence, that entail moral or legal guilt.

Negligence, in both law and morality, encourages people to have reasonable conceptions of their personal guilt, while at the same time enlarging the sphere of personal guilt to include some things that were not intended. It is crucial in modern life, especially with the increasing role of professionals in our society, that people de-velop such an expanded understanding of their personal respon-sibilities. For the omissions of professionals can be even more risk-producing than their commissions. In areas of great technological difficulty, such as medicine or engineering, it is often not possible for the average person to tell what services or products are haz-ardous. When medical and engineering professionals take risks with safety by their omissions, the potential for severe harm is quite large. It is thus important for people to have a sense of personal guilt for such omissions. A standard of negligence accomplishes this objective without a corresponding loss of a sense of personal guilt for one's harmful commissions.

SIX

Collective Inaction and Responsibility

To paraphrase something Edmund Burke once said: All that is necessary for evil to triumph in the world is for good people to do nothing. Great tragedies seem so overwhelming that they discourage people from working toward their resolution. In addition, to confront them as one's own responsibility means admitting that one's inactivity is connected to these tragedies. To do so involves a recognition that our lives are interconnected and interdependent in ways that run contrary to the myth that we have each gotten where we have by our own individual actions and without the help of others. To recognize this interconnectedness is to acknowledge that we have benefits, and also responsibilities, that extend beyond what we have done or could have done on our own.

World hunger and racial inequality are problems that individual persons cannot solve on their own. When faced with problems that must be resolved by collective action, people often feel no sense of personal responsibility, and hence they fail to do anything to solve the problems. But just as a person's inaction makes him or her at least partially responsible for harms that he or she could have prevented, so collective inaction of a group of persons may make the members of that group at least partially responsible for harms that the group could have prevented. This claim is especially important if there is not yet an organized group with a decision-making procedure, but instead what I will call a "putative group." Often, people could organize themselves into the kind of group that could prevent massive starvation or racial injustice. But the potential members of these groups often must first recognize that they share responsibility for the harms, in order to feel motivated to form structures allowing for collective action. Blame or feelings of guilt may not be appropriate in cases of collective inaction, but other less accusatory forms of responsibility may be appropriate, nonetheless.

Inaction leads to serious harm in the world, just as certainly as intentional, active wrongdoing. Yet inaction, especially collective inaction, presents difficult problems for theories of responsibility. These difficulties may be formulated in terms of two questions: Why, among the countless things people fail to do, should certain failures be singled out as constituting "collective inaction"? How should responsibility for the harmful consequences of these inactions be apportioned within a putative group? I address the first, conceptual question in section 2, and the second, normative question in section 3. In section 1, I explain why collective inaction raises conceptual and normative problems different from those raised by collective action.

The main thesis of this chapter is that if a harm has resulted from collective inaction, the degree of individual responsibility of each member of a putative group for the harm should vary based on the role each member could, counterfactually, have played in preventing the inaction. My thesis will be defended against two types of view: first, the view that individual responsibility for harms caused by collective inaction is the same as it would be if no reference were made to groups or putative groups; and, second, the view that individual responsibility for harms caused by collective inaction diminishes in proportion to the number of other members in the group or putative group. In section 4, I respond to several important practical and ontological objections that can be made against my views. And in the final section, I indicate why my views are especially important for the prevention of large-scale tragedies in contemporary times.

1. Collective Action and Collective Inaction

"Collective action" refers to the action of a collectivity. Collective action cannot necessarily be reduced to the aggregate personal actions of a group's members. If people can act collectively, and if there is some sense in calling their action intentional, then the group or collectivity is itself responsible for whatever harms result from its intentional actions. As I use these terms, *collective* responsibility concerns the nondistributed responsibility of a group of people structured in such a way that action can occur that could not occur if the members were acting outside the group.[1] On the other hand, *shared* responsibility concerns the aggregated responsibilities of individuals, all of whom contribute to a result and for that reason are personally responsible, albeit often to different degrees, for a given harmful result.

Even though collective responsibility is nondistributive, it often turns out that many members of a group that is collectively responsible for a harm are also personally responsible (or, as I will often say, share responsibility) for that harm. Consider the case of the downing of an Iranian passenger plane by U.S. military forces. Collective responsibility was attributed to the United States; but in addition, certain Americans, because of their participation, shared responsibility for what occurred. Since groups are composed of individuals, it is common for there to be both collective and shared responsibility for the same harm; but this is not necessary. A group may be collectively responsible for a harm and yet no member of the group individually shares responsibility for the harm.[2]

When a group is collectively responsible for a harm, the group as a whole must have done something or omitted to do something that played an important role in that harm. When a group or putative group fails to act and thereby contributes to a harm, it may be due to the fact that the group decided not to act or due to a lack of group decision. "Collective *omission*" refers to the failure of a group that collectively chooses not to act. "Collective *inaction*" refers to the failure to act of a collection of people that did not choose *as a group* to remain inactive but that could have acted as a group. "Collective inaction" is often a more appropriate term than "collective omission" for what occurs in putative groups. For collective omission, the group itself would have to refrain from performing a certain act, and that would involve some sort of decision by the group.[3] I believe that collective omissions, unlike collective inactions, can be treated much like collective actions. But I am most interested in those cases in which there is no decision-making structure on the basis of which it would otherwise be legitimate to claim that the group decided to do anything.

Collective inaction requires a conceptual analysis different from that required for collective action. In order to determine whether or not a group has engaged in collective *action,* one has to determine whether or not the group has in fact engaged in actions as a group, that is, actions that were facilitated by some aspect of the group's structure. In order to determine whether or not a putative group has engaged in collective *inaction,* one needs to determine whether or not a collection of people was, at a particular time, capable of acting

ɔ, even though it did not. For if these people were, at the
ɪpable of acting as a group, then any inaction should be un-
as merely the failure of the individuals to act. The mere ab-
sencͤ ∪ͥ action in a collection of people does not by itself mean that
there is a group that could have taken action. Likewise, the mere absence of action by a collection of people is not sufficient evidence
that there is a group that coheres enough to be the subject of collective responsibility. But a history of collective action by a group provides *prima facie* grounds for thinking that the putative group is
structured enough to be able to act collectively in some situations
and therefore to be the subject of collective responsibility for some of
its inactions.

Any collection of people, no matter how disparate the members'
interests may be, *could* develop a structure sufficient to allow it to
become a group capable of collective action. But for the retrospective
moral criticism of a collection of people for allowing a particular harm
to occur, what is necessary is that the collection of people could
have, and should have, developed the requisite structure *in time* to
act as a group at the moment. For negative moral assessment of the
harmful consequences of group inaction, it is required that a collection of people *should* have acted differently as a group. This implies
that it was plausible (not merely theoretically possible) that the collection of people could have so acted.

A business corporation has the kind of decision-making structure
that enables its members to act as a group. Some other groups are
able to accomplish intentional action because of solidarity of the
members, so that decisions can be reached even though there is no
formal decision-making procedure.[4] If people are able to decide how
to act as a group, and they decide not to act, then their failure to act
constitutes a collective omission. If people are able to decide how to
act as a group, but they do not reach any decisions, and as a result
nothing is done, then this is a clear case of collective inaction. But if
the collection of people has no previous history of collective action
or if it is not clear whether the collection could have reached a decision at the present, then it is not clear that the absence of action is an
instance of collective inaction, the consequences of which the group
is responsible for.

Thus, here is one clear reason for thinking that collective inaction
needs to be analyzed differently from collective action. In the face of
absence of action in a collection of people, as opposed to recognizable collective action, it cannot be determined whether a group ex-

ists that could, collectively, have acted otherwise. As a result, we don't yet know whether there is a group, which is itself the subject of collective responsibility, or whether it is only the individual members, as individuals, who are responsible, if anyone is. Analyzing collective inaction, unlike collective action, requires, among other things, posing a counterfactual question: Could the collection of people have avoided inaction? If they could not have avoided inaction, and if a given harm could have been prevented only by collective action, then the putative group would not be morally responsible for that harm.

Another important difference between collective action and collective inaction concerns the type of responsibility appropriate to attribute to the members of the groups in question. If a group engages in collective action that causes harm, then normally the members should feel guilt for their roles in this harm. But if a putative group participates in a harm through collective inaction, less accusatory forms of responsibility are relevant for its members. Since no decision was made by the group, and since the group had not assumed clearly defined roles in the community, it is not true that the group or its members intended to commit a wrong or negligently refrained from acting by remaining inactive. Therefore, feelings of shame or taint more appropriately follow from collective inaction than feelings of guilt, which find their appropriate locus concerning harms caused by collective action. I will return to this subject in section 4.

2. Collective Responsibility and Putative Groups

Throughout this chapter, I speak of putative groups, in which people are sometimes capable of acting in concert but in which no formal organization exists, and, as a result, there is no decision-making apparatus. It is not clear whether putative groups could, at a given time, take collective action. When a collection of persons has no decision-making structure, the inaction of these persons normally results at most in shared, rather than collective, responsibility. The major exception to this rule of thumb involves putative groups that could have developed a sufficient structure in time to avoid inaction. Concerning such cases, Virginia Held has proposed that: "The judgment, then, that 'Random Collectivity R is morally responsible for not constituting itself into a group capable of deciding upon an action,' is sometimes valid when it is obvious to a reasonable person that action rather than inaction is called for."[5] And

Robert Goodin has recently stated the same idea in somewhat different terms: "In the real world, it is these failures to organize [so as to coordinate individual action] to which collective responsibility most often attaches."[6]

Most authors who have considered the difficult issue of assigning responsibility to putative groups have relied on the strategy of assigning responsibility to these groups for not doing what is necessary to become structured enough to act, as a first step toward holding the group collectively responsible for the consequences of its inaction. But little else is normally said concerning how to determine if the putative group could have developed a decision mechanism or a mechanism of coordination in a short enough time to be able to prevent inaction in a given case. Rather, merely claiming that the putative group could have done so has seemed to be sufficient.[7]

In order to begin to distinguish among cases involving putative groups, consider a variation of one of the most discussed cases. A collection of bystanders on the shore hears the screams of a child in the cold, choppy waters hundreds of yards out to sea. No lifeguard is on duty. No single person present can save the child on his or her own; collective action is required to save the child. Yet the collection of bystanders does nothing, and the child drowns. It may seem that the mere possibility that this collection of people could have acted as a group is sufficient for assigning collective responsibility. However, it may be unrealistic to think that a collection of bystanders on a public beach could have formed into a life-saving brigade quickly enough (within minutes) to save a drowning child. To help in making such a determination, let us consider some factors that are normally important in the timely and decisive action of a group.

Leadership, solidarity, and intersubjective communication are well-known features of putative groups that have sufficient structure to act as a group. Each of these features provides a mechanism by which the individual intentions of the members of the group can be coordinated in such a way that purposeful action can be accomplished by group members acting together. These features set the stage for decision making which transforms the intentions of individuals into intentions and actions of the group as a whole.[8]

In the case of the people gathered on a beach observing a child drowning in choppy waters several hundred yards away, no single individual can save the drowning child. The ability to coordinate individual actions is necessary, and coordination needs to be accomplished very quickly if the group is to save the child's life. If the only commonality of these bystanders is that each happens to be on the beach on this particular day, it may be implausible to say that their failure to act constitutes collective inaction. Of course, there may be individual inactions, which are themselves blameworthy.

Contrast the case of the bystanders on the shore with that of people who learn of a famine in the Sudan and yet do nothing to try to aid the famine's victims. This collection of people also lacks the features necessary for intentional action as a group, but there is time to develop the mechanisms in order at least to save those who are not yet starving. Just as in the beach case, some persons in the collection may be able, because of their various leadership skills, to be more effective than others in bringing these people to form a group able to act intentionally. Yet there is enough time in the famine case to think that group formation is plausible, especially given that there is already a history of the timely development of just such relief operations. Since the collection of people who learn about the outbreak of famine in the Sudan can act collectively to prevent at least some of the potential harms from resulting, the putative group is *prima facie* collectively responsible for the harms that result, in part, from the group's inaction.

Even when there is plenty of time, there must be the practical possibility of developing coordination or decision making. Often quite a bit can be learned by looking at the histories of similar groups. During some famines, too little time elapsed from the time people learned about the problem, for example in June, until all the harms occurred, in July, for an effective relief effort to be mounted. Even though the collection of people might have been able in other cases to act as a group, they were not responsible for failing to take steps in June to prevent the harms of July. But in other cases, history will indicate that the people could have done something collectively in June, when they learned of the famine, to prevent harm from occurring in August. As a result, those people may be collectively responsible for the harmful consequences of their collective inaction. No rescue was possible in August, once June had passed with no organizational activity; nonetheless, these people might be collectively responsible for the August famine deaths because of what they could have done in June to form themselves into an organized group that could have prevented the harms in August.

Collective inaction does not merely involve aggregated individual inaction, with the mere possibility that collective action could have occurred. For inaction to be collective there must be some sense in which a group was not formed that could have been formed. There must be practical plausibility to the counterfactual claim that there could have been a group that, as a group, could have acted otherwise. If this condition is met, and if it is determined that a group should have acted, then the people are collectively responsible for harms resulting from their inaction. And this also has an importance for the assessment of individual responsibility, as we will next discover.

3. Sharing Responsibility for Collective Inaction

There are two standard views of how to distribute responsibility among the members of a putative group that has, due to inaction, contributed to a certain consequence. In one view, existence of the putative group makes no difference at all, and the members are responsible in the same way as if they had failed to act on their own and no one else had been present. In the other view, individual responsibility in a putative group is diminished in proportion to the number of members of the group. Neither of these views, I will argue, takes account of the concept of collective inaction I developed above. According to my view, if a putative group has engaged in collective inaction, then this makes the assignment of individual responsibility different than if the individuals have engaged in inaction on their own; but differential shares of responsibility are, nonetheless, not determined in proportion to the number of people who constituted, or could have constituted, the group.

Some thinkers argue that the fact that a putative group of people has failed to act does not affect the assignment of responsibility; each person is responsible for what he or she would have been responsible for if there had been no group. Even if the failure to act of each of several members of a group was necessary for the harm to occur, each person's responsibility should not be different just because others failed as well.[9] The argument normally advanced by these theorists is that either each person's inaction was the result of an intentional decision, and hence potentially blameworthy whether or not there was, or could have been, a group, or some of the members acted unintentionally, in which case they may be relieved of blame, just as they would be in any purely individual case of unintentional behavior. But this argument fails to consider a third alternative: a person's intentions are often influenced by others in the group, even in very loosely structured groups, and thus it sometimes makes sense to view the individual's responsibility in a group as different from what it would be if there were no group.

The psychologists John M. Darley and Bibb Latane constructed an experiment in which a person was ushered into a room for a discussion, which was held over an intercom system. Over the course of the discussion one of the participants underwent what appeared to be an epileptic seizure. The results of the study were that the likelihood a person would report an emergency situation varied, based on whether the person believed he or she was alone or in a group. "Eighty-five percent of the subjects who thought they alone knew of the victim's plight reported the seizure before the victim was cut off; only 31% of those who thought that four other bystanders were present did so."[10] Other studies indicate that individual intentions are shaped and changed in highly organized groups such as corporations, as well as in loosely structured groups such as mobs.

In putative groups, the determination of whether there is collective action is a counterfactual determination, in that it is based on whether individual decisions to be inactive could have been influenced by the involvement of other members. If the involvement of others could have made a difference, then we should not continue to assign responsibility to the members as if the group, or putative group, did not exist. As we saw in chapter 4, groups or collections of people can have a profound impact on the values of the members, thus warranting differential treatment of people in these groups than would be true otherwise.

But this does not mean that we should accept the other most prevalent view of these matters, namely, that responsibility in groups should be proportional to group size. Since there is no strict proportionality between the number of persons in a group and the way the members decide to form their intentions, there is no initial reason to think that responsibility should be apportioned in anything like equal shares based on the number of people present in the group. For some members play, or could have played, a more significant role in shaping or changing intentions than other members. Indeed, some members of a group or putative group are able, due to their leadership and persuasion skills, to cause other group members to do precisely the opposite of what they would have decided to do on their own.

Consider again the case of the bystanders on the beach who witness a child drowning in choppy waters out to sea. Most of these individuals would probably not risk their lives to attempt to save the child. Given that the rescue venture needs more than one person, few, if any, individuals would feel personally motivated to initiate action on their own. But when there is a collection of individuals, there may be people who have the kind of interpersonal skills that can be used to persuade other members to undertake the joint ventures which they would be reluctant to do without the persuasion. In such cases, the fact that people are not isolated from each other but are members of a putative group is relevant for judgments about inaction and responsibility, but not merely because of the size of the group.

If a collection of people can take collective action, then when they fail to act it makes sense to say that they have engaged in collective inaction. This fact will have an effect on the way responsibility for the consequences of such inaction should be distributed or shared within the putative group. Those who could have played leadership roles normally have a greater share in the responsibility than those who lack leadership or persuasion skills. Similarly, those who play the most important leadership roles in an organized group's collective action have a greater share in the responsibility for harmful collective action perpetrated by the group than do those who merely follow orders.

Greater or lesser shares of responsibility should not necessarily be understood by using the analogy of slices of a pie. I do not believe that the shares of some must be diminished just because it is determined that another person's responsibility has increased. I am not assuming that the sum total of shares of responsibility will necessarily remain fixed. And while I endorse the view espoused by Jonathan Cohen, that "no one is morally required to take on more than his fair share of a burden,"[11] a person's fair share is not merely determined by dividing the total number of people who have shares into the amount of responsibility to be assigned for the harm. It may be fair to require people to do as much as people in their positions can reasonably be expected to do, especially in emergency situations. And here, those who are more capable, due to their leadership skills, will have greater shares without necessarily diminishing the shares that others have, since the capacities of the others have not been diminished by the capacities of the leaders.

Two questions inevitably arise. Why should we place a greater burden on those who have leadership and persuasion skills? Why should those who lack such skills and who also play a necessary role in the inaction be less responsible than those who have leadership

114

skills but, due to other factors, play no role? It might be claimed that those who have leadership or persuasion skills should not be singled out for a greater share in responsibility for the consequences of collective inaction, since they do not exercise these skills in any way that makes a contribution to the group's inaction. Or it might be claimed that it is a mistake to hold people who have leadership skills up to higher moral standards than those who lack those skills.

To address these objections it will help to consider the notion of "contribution" in cases of inaction. Just as in cases involving action, those who play necessary roles in an inaction do not always play the same roles. The ringleader of a mob plays a more important role in mob violence than someone who follows his lead, even though the violence in question requires the concerted action of all of the members of the mob. In this case, it is plausible to say that the ringleader's role is doubly necessary. The violence requires the actions of all the members, and the ringleader is one of these members. In addition, without the ringleader's leadership, the other members would not feel motivated to do their parts. Since the actions of the ringleader are doubly necessary, it is often appropriate to assign a greater share of responsibility to him or her. Similarly, those who could take leadership roles in preventing inaction, but do not do so, play two necessary roles in the ensuing collective inaction, and may be appropriately assigned a greater share of responsibility for its consequences than other members of a group.

From a different perspective, it might be claimed that some individuals should not have less responsibility than others due to factors of which they were not aware, such as the leadership skills of other members, especially if these factors did not play a role in changing the results of the individuals' inaction.[12] This objection again calls attention to the notion of contribution. Consider a situation in which a number of people know an important fact about a person being investigated by the government, and each decides to say nothing to the investigators. If each person on his or her own decides to keep quiet, and if each person's silence is necessary for the deceit to occur, then it appears that each person is equally to blame for whatever harm the deceit causes. Since each contributes to the silence and each person's contribution is necessary, there is no reason, so this argument would suggest, to treat one person differently from another. This seems especially plausible since none of them is aware of what the others are doing or not doing.

But this is not a good analogy for cases of collective inaction. Collective inaction of a putative group occurs because all (or some) of the members fail to act, but also because those who could influence the group to take action do not exert their influence. Understood in this way, the aggregate silence of the people in the government investigation case is not clearly an example of collective inaction. The example concerns isolated individuals, each of whom can break the silence and prevent the group's inaction. No collective action is called for, since each person can remain silent on his or her own, and hence the morally relevant fact is not whether the putative group can act collectively or not, but whether any of the members can act otherwise. This is an example of aggregate inaction, not collective inaction. When collective inaction occurs, responsibility will vary based on the roles people could, counterfactually, have played in bringing the putative group to act.

It may be further objected that by increasing the responsibilities of some of the members who could have played leadership roles, the door is opened for other members to feel that they need not concern themselves as much about preventing harm as they might otherwise. This may result, so the objection runs, in a further diminution of many people's sense of individual responsibility. The rejoinder "I'm not to blame for the fact that others did nothing" will be used by some individuals to ward off any attempt to suggest that as a member of a putative group, individuals should still retain a personal sense of guilt when their group acts wrongly. However, differential shares of responsibility should not translate into absence of responsibility on the part of any members of the putative groups we have been considering. Individuals still share responsibility for the harm caused by inaction in such cases. But the extent of the personal responsibility of each member nonetheless varies, based on the role that each individual could have played in bringing the putative group to take action instead of remaining inactive.

4. Practical and Ontological Objections

I have defended the following two principles governing moral responsibility in putative groups:

1. A putative group of people engages in the kind of inaction that warrants collective responsibility if:
   (a) the members of the group fail to act to prevent a harm, the prevention of which would have re-

quired the coordinated actions of (some of) the members of the group;

(b) it is plausible to think that the group could have developed a sufficient structure in time to allow the group to act collectively to prevent the harm; and

(c) it is reasonable to think that the members of the group should have acted to prevent the harm rather than doing anything else, such as preventing other harms which they also could have prevented.

2. The share of individual responsibility of each group member varies, based on the role that each member could have played in bringing the putative group to prevent the harm, if:

(a) the group is collectively responsible for the effects of its inaction; and

(b) the ability of the group to act to prevent the harm was based on the leadership, persuasion, etc., characteristics of one (or some) of the members.

These principles will allow us to ascertain how to address difficult questions of individual responsibility in putative groups.

There are two sorts of objections that can be raised against my claims about collective inaction and shared responsibility. In what follows I will try to bolster and clarify my claims by responding to several important practical and ontological problems. I should say at the beginning that my claims are meant to be provocative in two senses of that term. First, I am attempting to push to the limit our conceptions of agency and responsibility, to see whether or not it is a mistake to set the limits of responsibility at the relatively modest levels at which one is only responsible for what one directly causes. Second, I am attempting to inspire people to see the potential for great social good that can be achieved when they think about collective, rather than individual, solutions to social problems. Since this chapter is meant to be both conceptually and morally provocative, it is no surprise that strong positions will be taken in opposition to it.

Before beginning, I would like to point out that some groups, such as OXFAM, have managed both to alleviate suffering from particular famines and to provide research and long-term aid toward the elimination of the causes of famine in regions of the world where famine has been most prone to break out. OXFAM is also a good example of an organization that was begun and is sustained by individuals who see the importance of collective action toward the resolution of world hunger. Even given the enormity of the problem of world hunger, there are rather simple things people can do that will make at least some difference; setting up local chapters of OXFAM is relatively easy to do. It is often only our collective inaction that stands in the way of dealing with large social problems.

I will turn first to practical and moral issues. It might be objected that my view of collective inaction has a problem which is similar to the problem concerning individual inaction. There are simply far too many harms that any person could have acted (with others) to prevent to think that an individual is responsible for all of the harms he or she failed to prevent. A person would have to spend all of his or her time engaged in the prevention of harm and would have no time at all for more positive pursuits of personal life plans. Similarly, it might be said that my proposal would require collections of people to spend all of their time trying to prevent harm, leaving no time for the pursuit of positive plans. Indeed, putative groups would have to spend all of their time merely reacting to the world, perhaps going from famine to famine, rather than trying to do something positive to end the conditions that give rise to starvation from famine.

Talking about shared responsibility for collective inaction is a way of calling attention to the need for people to look beyond their individual lives, to consider what they could accomplish in their communities through joint action. Such a proposal does not yet say which actions should be taken, when there are several that are possible, nor which harms should be prevented. Once people have expanded their conscious awareness of their larger responsibilities, then they should feel motivated to try, through some political process, to determine which harms are the ones that should be tackled first. In the previous chapter I suggested that one way to reach such decisions is for the individual to think about what it would be reasonable to expect of someone relevantly like that individual. Such a strategy would place emphasis on the roles one has assumed.

The key to limiting the extent of one's responsibility for collective inaction lies in an understanding of the range of omissions that a group is most responsible for. In general, an individual person is most responsible for those omissions that are somehow connected to what that person has previously done or to expectations he or she has raised. Likewise, putative groups are most responsible for preventing harms that those groups have done something to bring about, or about which they have raised expectations. The next most important set of harms are those that a putative group is uniquely positioned to prevent. In general, it is the roles that people have in society, and the opportunities and expectations attached to those roles, that set the reasonable limits on our responsibilities concerning collective inaction.

Whether a putative group should hold itself, or be held, morally responsible for failing to prevent a particular harm, as opposed to some other harm it could have prevented, is something that will have to be determined by what people feel to be most reasonable; the details of this assessment may vary from society to society. But responsibility assessments should not be merely a function of what particular people happen to think. Morality should have the role of inspiring and criticizing, as well as partially reflecting, existing norms. When people come to realize that there are serious harms in their societies that they can prevent through the formation of groups, then they should also decide in as reasonable a manner as possible which harms are the most serious and hence which harms they should direct their attention toward first.

Why should the prevention of harm be one of the main moral requirements people concern themselves with? The duty to prevent harm is a subcategory of the duty to prevent or relieve suffering.[13] Both of these duties are intimately connected to the duty of due care we discussed in the previous chapter. The duty to prevent harm is a duty all persons have. It is the duty upon which more stringent duties, such as the duty not to kill, are based. All societies recognize some version of the duty to prevent harm, although there is wide disagreement about what constitutes harm. The interpretation of the duty to prevent harm, like that of the duty of due care, will vary from community to community and will generally be limited by what is considered reasonable in a specific community.

In cases of individual negligence, people are considered responsible for their omissions or inaction if they had a duty to act. In most cases these duties are determined by the roles people voluntarily assume in a given community. In cases of collective inaction, we are considering roles a person *could* have played in directing the actions of a putative group as partially determinative of the person's responsibility. In these cases, a person's inaction cannot be treated as strictly analogous to a person's chosen action, since these people may not be aware of the roles they could have played. Of course, once one is aware of the things that one could do, and one then does not do them, then lack of action is something one has chosen.

A person's role in an organized group is not strictly analogous to a

119

person's role in the kind of putative groups I have been considering. But even putative groups have individuals who are, or could be, leaders. Such groups exist within communities, and most communities have certain individuals who are recognized as, and recognize themselves as, leaders of the community. Of course, these people do not often have clearly specified "official roles" in the putative groups of which they are members, or of which they could be members. But there are leadership roles that some can play and others cannot.

Moral responsibility is a scaler concept; there are degrees of responsibility. Responsibility is well suited to agency, for agency also admits of degree. Group inaction is a partial cause of serious harms in our society. Other factors may be greater causes; and when "official duties" are violated, there is clearly a cause with greater moral weight. But I believe it is undeniable that inaction can and does play some causal role in some harms. The question then becomes: What does partial agency mean for moral assessment? I have argued in several places that if one is the partial cause of a harm, then one should have partial moral responsibility for it. But partial responsibility normally does not entail guilt. Rather, less accusatory assessments should follow cases of less than full responsibility.

In the cases we have been considering, in which the failure of many people to act is involved, shared responsibility normally does not entail guilt. Shame, though, is directly related to a person's conception of herself or himself, rather than to explicit behavior (which is what guilt most commonly attaches to). Because shame concerns the self's identity, it is more appropriately felt than guilt when one's group fails to prevent a harm, since it is the association between the group's identity and one's own that generates the moral feelings, rather than what one has directly done. But since one's group associations are generally things one can do something about, they may generate responsibility and with it corresponding moral feelings. Shame seems to fit the bill here, and as I argue in a later chapter, so does moral taint.

Shame fits the diffuse examples of collective inaction better than guilt does. As W. H. Walsh observes: "There are occasions on which we take pride in, or feel shame about, things which are in no sense our personal doing." Of course, not all feelings of shame are appropriate. But shame is nonetheless much more closely connected to the actions of one's group than is guilt. Walsh further states: "Morals supplements law by bringing softer and subtler pressures to bear, pressures which affect a man not just in his personal capacity but also through his relatives, friends and associates."[14] In talking about shared responsibility, I am urging that we think about these "softer and subtler pressures" associated with shame (and moral taint) rather than the harsher, more legalistic, pressures associated with guilt (and blame).

In my account of collective inaction, shame is what people should feel when groups to which they belong have failed to prevent harm that should have been prevented. These people should feel shame literally, in the sense that they should want to hide their faces, to regret that they are members of the groups in question. As I will later argue, such feelings of shame or moral taint should cause people to seek to change the behavior of their groups or to disassociate themselves from their groups.

Within this orientation, it is plausible to say that some people, those who could play certain leadership roles, have more responsibility (in terms of shame or taint rather than guilt) than those who could not assume such roles. Why? Because, I believe, it is plausible to expect more of such people than of others. As I have argued, the amount of responsibility for failure to meet these expectations is quite a bit less than the amount or type of responsibility that would apply if the leadership roles were clearly defined and then straightforwardly avoided by the persons who are said to be negligent. But I will certainly admit that there are many disanalogies between the kind of roles I am discussing and roles that exist in organized groups a person has voluntarily joined. I will say much more about roles and shared responsibility in the last two chapters of this book.

Ontologically, one might raise the challenge that it is difficult if not impossible to individuate the putative groups I have been discussing. The boundary separating one putative group, which could do something about world hunger, from another putative group, which could do something about racial inequalities, is fuzzy at best. And the identification of a group that could do something about world hunger does raise thorny problems concerning possible worlds. Let me attempt to say something about this point, again by reference to the example of OXFAM. There is an overdetermination of the group that could alleviate some of the world hunger problem in the way OXFAM has. The possible members of such a group far outnumber the actual number needed to get the thing off the ground and do some good. But with a problem of the size of world hunger, it would take many OXFAM-like groups, involving millions of people, before any further increase in effort would be wasted effort. While the exact contours of the group remain fuzzy, overdetermination is not as significant a problem as one might have initially thought.

Furthermore, one might raise the ontological challenge that there is something suspicious going on when it is claimed that what people are initially held responsible for is failing to organize. The act of organizing is itself an act. If there is enough of a group present to be responsible for not forming an organization, why isn't there enough of a group to be responsible for the harms it allows by its inactivity? Because of difficulty in answering these questions one might be forced to conclude that the groups I discuss are largely fictive. What is the point in calling such loose putative groups "groups" at all?

In the beach case, the difference between a *random collection* of bystanders and a *putative group* of bystanders is that in the putative group there is enough potential leadership for the group to constitute itself relatively quickly into an organized group and hence later to perform collective action. Initially, the people on the beach cannot perform collective action, since they lack a mechanism by which to accomplish coordinated intentional behavior. But given a demonstration of one person's leadership abilities, they are not merely a random collection of people. For they can, under the leadership of that person, develop an organizational structure, so that *later* they can engage in collective action. But at the *present*, the most the group can do is to form itself into an organized group. The putative group is not fictive in the way a random collection of people is fictively referred to as a group. We can and do make sense of such talk of putative groups, both from an ontological and a moral point of view.

5. Tragedy and Inactivity

It is common to appeal to a variation of Kant's famous doctrine, that "ought" implies "can," to argue that a person should not be held responsible for a harm he or she could not have prevented. Since many major harms, such as world hunger and racial inequality, require collective action for resolution, an individual does not feel motivated to do anything about them, since he or she could not, acting alone, do anything about them. In addition, at the time such harms occur, it is often true that even people acting together cannot do anything to prevent them. For in these cases there were things that had to be done earlier in order for people, even acting collectively, to be able to act effectively in the present. Such facts provide impetus for people to deny that they are responsible, in any sense, for such harms. I have tried to provide a framework for responding to such positions.

When the interrelations among putative group members have made, or could have made, a causal difference, then ascriptions of collective responsibility are appropriate, not just aggregate individual responsibility. This means that different members of the putative group may have different degrees of shared moral responsibility. In the putative groups we have been considering, those members who could contribute at all are at least partially responsible for the consequences of collective inaction. And in addition, the leaders of the putative group, that is, those who clearly could have led the group, bear a greater-than-normal share of responsibility for the consequences of collective inaction. In any event, people should not feel an absence of responsibility in such cases just because the problem at issue was not something an individual could have solved on his or her own. Many people share responsibility for a tragedy such as world hunger, because of both what they have done to contribute to the tragedy and what they have not done, in combination with others, to prevent it.

In the last three chapters I have argued that sharing responsibility is appropriate in some cases when omission or inaction of group members contributes to a harm. In chapter 4, I indicated how it is that membership in groups often changes the values and attitudes on the basis of which individuals approach potentially harmful situations. Value transformation in groups binds people together and affects personal responsibility in two ways. First, since the members of groups often come to share attitudes and values, especially concerning their willingness to risk certain kinds of harm, they also share responsibility for these harms. Second, given this transformation of values and attitudes, members of a group should be vigilant in preventing harms within the group. When they do not try to prevent harms that are made more likely by the existence of the group, then they come to share responsibility for these harms.

In chapter 5, I argued that the members of certain groups who do not act to prevent certain harms from occurring may be guilty for these harms due to their negligence. Members of professional groups should be vigilant in acting to prevent harm, since the public has relied on such expectations. But also, members of groups who have assumed various roles designed to prevent harm within the group, such as those who have assumed supervisory roles, should be more vigilant than others in their behavior. In both cases, failure to act vigilantly in the prevention of harm is often correctly judged to be negligent. A person's negligence is one of the most straightforward bases for the judgment that the person shares responsibility for harms he or she has not directly caused. The social existentialist account of shared responsibility I have developed comes closest in these cases to matching the way that most people already regard their responsibilities.

In the present chapter, though, I advanced the controversial thesis that people also share responsibility for harms their putative group could have prevented, but did not, due to collective inaction. In a sense, this position is only the natural extension of the arguments I advanced in earlier chapters. Its plausibility depends both on accepting the legitimacy of the concept of shared responsibility and on understanding shared responsibility as sometimes entailing personal shame or taint rather than guilt or blame. In these various discussions I have been guided by the insight that people should have increased responsibilities that correlate with the increased benefits they derive from group membership.

Great social tragedies are made more likely due to our attitudes and our failures to act collectively. Even seemingly minor matters, such as attitudes and inaction, can greatly increase the likelihood that groups and individuals will cause harm. If our communities are to become safer and more humane, people will need to feel an increased sense of shared responsibility for what their fellow community members do. In the final chapters of this book, I turn more explicitly to the subject of what a community is and how one's role in a community should affect one's sense of responsibility.

PART THREE

Communities, Roles, and Responsibilities

—

SEVEN

Philosophers and Political Responsibility

It is often claimed that physicians should be held to a higher-than-normal standard of conduct concerning the foreseeable but unintended harmful consequences of aiding roadside traffic victims. Physicians are expected to know quite a bit about the risks of even their well-intentioned acts. If a physician moves a seriously injured person, thereby aggravating that person's injury, then the physician should feel, or be held, responsible for the added injury, even though the average bystander should not feel, or be held, responsible for the very same harm. Bystanders are not expected to know about the risks, whereas physicians are. In the following chapters, I will examine the relationship between social roles and responsibility. I will begin with an extended example drawn from the domain I know best, professional philosophy, asking what political responsibilities philosophers have as a result of their roles within society. Next (in chapter 8), I turn to the more general subject of the moral responsibilities that follow from being a member of a community. And I conclude with a discussion (in chapter 9) of some of the problems that result when one's moral responsibilities are too closely identified with the role expectations within given communities. As in the previous chapters, I argue for an expanded domain of moral responsibility, but I also address the question of what limits need to be imposed on the notion of role responsibility.

Recently, a debate has been raging about whether philosophers should be held to a higher-than-normal standard of conduct concerning the foreseeable but unintended harmful political consequences of their writings or their participation in various political events. While recent revelations about Martin Heidegger's involvement in the Nazi Party have spurred this debate, the issue is clearly much larger than such political actions of leading philosophers. For most of us, the issue is whether there is any reason to be concerned at all about the possible political repercussions of our philosophizing. The larger question, of which this is only one part, is: What are the political responsibilities of philosophers? I shall set the stage for answering this question by considering philosophers as academic professionals, as writers, and as members of socially esteemed associations. Throughout this chapter, my concern is to examine the profession of philosophy to see whether philosophers have special duties, such as stimulating the public or pursuing wisdom, that might reduce their political responsibilities. It is the thesis of this chapter that philosophers have heightened rather than diminished political responsibilities due to the nature of their work.

In a plenary address to the Eleventh Inter-American Congress of Philosophy, Richard Rorty reopened an old controversy in the history of philosophy. Rorty declared:

> We should not assume, that it is our task, as professors of philosophy, to be the avant-garde of political movements. We should not ask, say, Davidson or Gadamer, for the "political implications" of their view of language, nor spurn their work because of a lack of such implications. . . . We should discard . . . Heidegger's idea that the fortunes of philosophy determine the fortunes of mankind.[1]

Rorty has been criticized from various circles, especially for his insensitivity in making such claims in the Third World, where philosophers often think of themselves as, and actually become, politically astute critics of their societies.[2] In this context, Rorty's attempt to defend philosophy as a form of "play," which has political significance, if at all, only in that it provides political hopes in the form of utopian speculations, was especially poignant. I hope to provide a philosophical challenge to the claims of Rorty and others that philosophers should not be seen as having heightened political responsibilities. First, though, I will counter the two most common claims for the diminished responsibility of philosophers. Then, I will offer a positive argument for philosophers' heightened political responsibilities. And at the end, I will offer a few remarks on the special responsibilities of philosophers as members of a professional group.

1. The Philosopher as Gadfly

In Plato's *Apology*, Socrates defends the value of his philosophizing in the following terms:

If you kill me you will not easily find another like me. I was attached to the city by the god—though it seems a ridiculous thing to say—as upon a great and noble horse which was somewhat sluggish because of its size and needed to be stirred up by a kind of gadfly. It is to fulfill some such function that I believe the god has placed me in the city. I never cease to rouse each and every one of you, to persuade and reproach you all day long and everywhere I find myself in your company.[3]

The use of this metaphor to describe the role of the philosopher is especially telling. The gadfly's role (speaking anthropomorphically) is simply to stimulate the horse. Whatever means it takes to achieve this end, and whatever additional ends are achieved in the process of pursuing this primary end, are considered proper. The gadfly's responsibility is simply to stimulate the horse, to move it, kicking and screaming perhaps, out of its comfortable but sluggish state.

Socrates says that the philosopher's role in society is parallel to the gadfly's position on the horse. What the society ultimately does as a result of this stimulation is not the responsibility of the philosopher. Indeed, a bit later in the *Apology*, Socrates draws out this conclusion quite explicitly.

I am equally ready to question the rich and the poor if anyone is willing to answer my questions and listen to what I say. And I cannot justly be held responsible for the good or bad conduct of these people, as I never promised to teach them anything and have not done so. If anyone says he has learned anything from me, be assured that he is not telling the truth.[4]

Socrates argues that the only thing that could make him responsible for the public consequences of his teachings would be some sort of special obligation he incurred by virtue of promise or contract. But short of such special considerations, according to Socrates, the philosopher is not responsible for the effects of his or her teachings.

An analogous argument is often developed concerning the role of journalists. It is contended that the chief duty of journalists is to stimulate their audience by informing them of the facts. If the result of disseminating certain information is that harm occurs, the journalist, according to this view, is not responsible for that harm. If members of the public are stimulated to form vigilante gangs as the result of being informed by a journalist about allegations of wrongdoing by members of a minority group in a community, the ensuing harm is only an unintended consequence of the journalist's pursuit of his or her primary duty to keep the public informed. When journalists worry about the way certain people might react to information, so this argument continues, they are likely to engage in self-censure that will have the effect of making it impossible vigorously to provide the public with information, which professional journalists should regard as paramount.

For those professionals who have lower-than-normal responsibilities for harm, it is often claimed that they also have supposedly offsetting higher-than-normal obligations, for example, the obligation to pursue wisdom more vigorously than the normal citizen. I will take up the special obligation of philosophers to pursue wisdom in the next section. Let me here merely point out that all professionals are obligated to pursue some value or goal more diligently than nonprofessionals, but not even all professionals who engage in similar tasks have similarly lowered responsibilities. For example, philosophers and journalists are awarded status quite different from that of other authors or teachers. The Socratic position seems to be that there is something about stimulating people to think philosophically that makes even the explicitly formulated speeches and writings of philosophers off limits to political criticism. This argument does not necessarily apply to writers concerned with other kinds of stimulation.

To begin to assess Socrates' argument advanced above, I wish to turn to an example from contemporary times. Consider a situation I observed about twenty years ago at Hyde Park Speaker's Corner in London. Among the many speakers was a Pakistani who delivered an eloquent and thoughtfully constructed speech against the political philosophy of the Indian government. But as the speaker progressed, a large crowd of Indians gathered; many of them became quite agitated by the Pakistani's speech. Police arrived just as the crowd began to surge toward the speaker. Many arrests were made in the ensuing melee, and the Pakistani speaker was taken into police custody. Was he at least partially responsible for the near-riot, which was an easily predictable political reaction to his speech? Could he have used Socrates' defense and claimed that he had made no special commitment to the audience, other than to stimulate them?

I believe that the Pakistani speaker was at lest partially responsible, although possibly not blameworthy. He understood (or should have understood) that the crowd of Indians would respond in a violent way to his speech, and yet he did nothing to try to minimize these possibly harmful effects. As a result, he was at least partially responsible for the outcome. Of course, there may have been overridingly important considerations (such as the need to speak out against the repression of ethnic minorities by the Indian government) which made it true, all things considered, that the speaker did not act in a blameworthy way. But the issue before us in this example is not whether he was blameworthy, but rather whether he should have taken into account, and felt responsible for, the possible reaction by the crowd. It is this question that I think deserves a clearly positive answer, and that may serve as an analogy for some cases of philosophical speech and writing.

I will later argue that some philosophers should be treated like the speaker in the case above. But the case of Socrates is different. Socrates did not clearly cause foreseeable harm by his philosophizing, contrary to what his accusers claimed at his trial. If the harm that results from one's philosophizing was difficult to predict, then it is not true that one is responsible for that harm. But it is nonetheless true, contrary to what Socrates claimed, that philosophers should worry about the effects that are likely to occur as a result of their written or spoken words.

Even at Hyde Park Speaker's Corner, a speaker has the duty to minimize the harm likely to result from his or her speech. If the speaker had been a member of a profession that had assumed certain roles in the society concerning speeches, then the assessment of the case would be easier yet. Professional status carries with it role responsibilities that change the normal moral relations existing among members of a society. Role responsibilities are responsibilities one has by virtue of having agreed to take on a certain set of tasks in society, or perhaps by virtue of having been thrust not unwillingly into the position of assuming various tasks. At least for some roles, the key element is that one voluntarily undertakes various duties that one would not normally have. One is committed by voluntarily taking the position and the duties entailed by it. If harms result from failure to do those things a person has a professional duty to do, then the person is responsible for those harms. Professionals of all sorts have similar duties, generally understood under the label "due care," with respect to their professed realm of expertise. That is, professionals are expected to carry out their tasks in ways that cause minimal harm to others.[5]

Professionals are those, most basically, who profess to have specialized knowledge or skill that sets them apart from other members of a community. The roles professionals assume create privileges for them, and their increased responsibilities are linked to their privileged status in the society. A profession is different from an isolated task in that a profession carries with it a set of duties which last over the course of one's professional life, as a cost of having professional privileges, whereas the roles associated with discrete tasks are generally not things which define a realm of behavior for a lifetime. Role responsibility makes the most sense in the context of a relatively autonomous field of action. This is why those who are professional philosophers have responsibilities different from those who merely dabble in philosophy; and this is why those who are political philosophers should expect to have their speeches treated differently from those of people who occasionally make political speeches.

Philosophers, like all other professionals, achieve a privileged status in the society on the basis of successfully claiming to have expertise in a certain field of knowledge. This privileged status involves social esteem and monetary rewards, as well as recognition that philosophers are people whose opinions are to be afforded the high status of academic legitimacy. Part of the public's perception is due to the claims that philosophers make on behalf of their own discipline. Socrates denied that he had made any claim to expertise, but it seems clear that he did, nonetheless, attain quite a privileged position in his society and that he did much to cultivate this status. Today, the situation is even clearer. Few of us are itinerant philosophers who must go to the marketplace to contract with potential students and philosophical disciples. Most philosophers are employed by universities and colleges, and many philosophers are, in effect, paid by the state for the expertise they claim to have.

Today, unlike ancient Greek times, philosophers are publicly privileged through membership in their professional societies. There is a corresponding expectation that they will not betray this public trust. Just as the Pakistani speaker should have worried about the likely effects of his speech, so any philosopher today should worry about the possible harmful effects of his or her philosophizing. Of course, it is possible to consider or even worry about these potentially harmful effects and yet to decide there are other overriding factors that allow one justifiably to philosophize anyway. The point is that one should take such considerations into account and be motivated by them.

While philosophers today, just as in Socrates' time, make no explicit promises about the probable effects of their teachings, it is nonetheless true that there are reasonable expectations affecting responsibility, which are largely fueled by the conduct of philosophers. It is reasonable to expect, for example, that philosophers will try to stimulate their societies in ways that are, on balance, positive, and that they will take care to minimize harm to the members of those societies, with the possible exception of harm inevitably resulting from a strategy producing great good. These expectations follow from the status that philosophers are granted in society, just as is true for any profession. The lack of vigilant oversight of professional behavior by members of the public, as we will see in section 3, is also an important moral consideration related to the issue of reasonable expectation. Before addressing that issue, I will examine the most common argument in support of the lowered political responsibilities of philosophers.

2. The Philosopher as Seeker of Wisdom

Since Greek times, it has been claimed that philosophers are those best situated to seek wisdom, but that this pursuit will be hampered if philosophers need to concern themselves with what will be done with the wisdom they uncover. There is an analogy with contemporary arguments on behalf of research in the field of nuclear physics. If physicists had had to worry about what others might do with nuclear fusion, so it is claimed, one of the most important scientific discoveries of the twentieth century would have been impeded.

In 1968, in the midst of the terrific turmoil on college campuses caused in part by active support of the Vietnam War by various university professors, the philosopher William Earle argued that philosophers could not properly pursue their professional duties if they had to worry about politics.[6] Earle claimed that the chief duty of a philosopher is to pursue his or her "area of verifiable and teachable knowledge." But this area is distinct from ideology, and really can only be pursued if philosophers eschew considerations of ideology and "life experiences" altogether.

Very similar arguments are often made on behalf of other professionals. For example, it is claimed that lawyers have the chief duty of providing the strongest possible defense of their clients. Only in this way, so it is claimed, can there be justice in society. But if lawyers must concern themselves with possible ancillary harms that occur due to the defense of their clients, it will be impossible to serve their primary duty. If, for instance, lawyers adversely affect the reputation of those whom they must call as witnesses in order properly to defend their clients, this harm is, even if foreseen, not something for which lawyers are responsible.[7]

Alan Goldman provides the general form of such arguments, stressing the notion that most professions have special roles, which actually reduce their normal moral responsibilities and shield the professional from certain forms of common criticism:

> Certain other charges of misconduct in business and the professions are defended by appeal to special professional goals, norms and roles: the need to pursue profit for business managers, the requirement to place clients' interests first for lawyers, or to prolong life itself for doctors. Such disputes relate often to the well-meaning behavior of professionals in pursuit of the fundamental values of their professions.[8]

The key to this defense against the charge of professional responsibility for harm is the claim that the pursuit of these special roles or duties *necessarily* requires the disregard of certain potential harms. Thus, according to this argument, professionals are relieved of responsibility for harms that members of the general population would normally be held responsible for.

Should philosophers have the resolve to pursue wisdom wherever it leads them, even if great harm is risked by such pursuit? Is it the professional duty of philosophers to pursue all that might be called wisdom, and do philosophers therefore have a corresponding exemption from the ordinary person's responsibility to pursue only those options that involve, at most, a minimum of harm? And if philosophers do have such a professional status, what justification can be offered in support of this status?

It is now time to get down to some cases. Consider the writings of Friedrich Nietzsche. In a large number of places, Nietzsche makes remarks which could easily be interpreted as anti-Semitic. Both in Nietzsche's own time and later, his writings were used to justify the actions of those who wanted to exterminate the Jewish race. Walter Kaufmann has tried to defend Nietzsche by pointing out that quite often Nietzsche follows a remark that could be seen as anti-Semitic with an explanation that makes another interpretation more likely.[9] Nonetheless, the reaction to his writings by the anti-Semites of his time is surely something Nietzsche could have foreseen. Nietzsche's writings clearly fueled the growing movement of violence toward Jews. This was no aberrant response, for Nietzsche was clearly aware of the climate of his times, which increasingly held Jews in contempt. If his writings had been unambiguously pro-Semitic, and yet they still fueled anti-Semitism, things would have been different. But Nietzsche intentionally wrote in a way which admitted of many interpretations. I want to argue that Nietzsche cannot be relieved of responsibility for anti-Semitic violence spurred on by his writings simply by the claim that his writings were a necessary part of his pursuit of philosophical truth.

Responsibility is closely linked to roles and to causation, but responsibility is a wider category than blame. Nietzsche's role as a philosopher, and the causal influence of his writing on anti-Semitic violence, make him at least partially responsible for that violence. Nonetheless, there may be other facts that make it true that Nietzsche is not to be blamed for this violence. For blameworthiness involves a consideration of moral factors other than roles and causation; for instance, what people intend to do, what other people are doing or should be doing, what other values are at stake. In this chapter I leave questions of blame largely unresolved. Philosophers and other professionals should hold themselves responsible for foreseeable harmful effects of their professional work, but they are not necessarily to be blamed if others choose to act harmfully as a result of that professional work. Rather, as I suggest in the next chapter, feelings of shame or taintedness are more appropriate in such cases.

Let us next consider the notion of causing harm, which has played a central role in the discussion so far. It is common to distinguish between proximate and remote causation.[10] Proximate causation, understood by reference to responsibility or liability, involves that last human act standing in a chain of events leading up to a harmful result. I assume that philosophers are quite likely to be both responsible and blameworthy when they are the proximate causes of harm. But philosophers may also stand in a causal chain that leads to harm, when other human agents are the direct causes of harm. These examples of remote or indirect influence are harder to assess, especially if the others who directly cause harm have in some sense chosen to do so. Nietzsche's writings were most likely only an indirect cause of the violence inflicted against Jews in turn-of-the-century Germany. If these harms were foreseeable, then Nietzsche may have been indirectly responsible for them. But those who were the direct causes of the harm, if they chose to act unjustifiably, are those to whom blame should be assigned.

I agree that philosophers should have the resolve to pursue wisdom wherever it leads them, but this does not mean that they are relieved of responsibility for the harms that are foreseeable and clearly likely to be caused, even remotely, by that pursuit. Similarly, the physician is not completely relieved of responsibility for the foreseeable but remote harms that result from operations performed so as to save a patient's life. If Nietzsche's writings contributed to anti-Semitic violence, then he is not relieved of responsibility simply because his writings had as their primary emphasis the pursuit of truth. The great positive value of the goals these professionals serve should be seen as an important, but not necessarily an overriding, factor in the assessment of responsibility for harms they may cause. Unless it is clear that most philosophers will stop pursuing wisdom if they are to be responsible for some of the harms that result from this pursuit, my proposal is not affected by the above worries. It is likewise true in medicine that most physicians will continue to pursue the goal of healing the sick, even though they are responsible for some of the harms that result from this pursuit.

Only when it does seem clear that professionals will stop pursuing their professional goals, it is important to ask whether they should continue to be responsible for things for which the non-professional is not responsible. And then we would need to weigh the value of the goals of the particular profession against the harm likely to occur from the pursuit of professional goals. Many have proposed that "professional" boxing be outlawed because its entertainment value is simply not great enough to override the harm to participants and, by the example boxing sets, to members of the society at large. The attempt to outlaw such practices results from the knowledge that the practices themselves cannot be conducted if the practitioners are responsible for the harms that are likely to result. But most activities are not of this sort; the people who engage in the activity can hold themselves, or be held, responsible for certain harms without risking the destruction of the activity itself.

Even for those activities that would be destroyed if the people performing them were held responsible for the ensuing harms, in general this is not sufficient in order to show that the people *should* not be held, or hold themselves, responsible. In addition, it must be shown that it would be a worse thing not to have that occupation or profession and thus not to have the attendant risks of harm, than it would be to have the occupation or profession and also to have the attendant risks of harm. The defenders of the overriding value of philosophy must meet this additional requirement if they are to sustain their arguments. Yet surely such a defense cannot be accomplished in the abstract. It must be undertaken on a case-by-case basis, since without specific knowledge of the harms that are risked, a judgment cannot be made concerning whether the risks are outweighed by the value of a philosopher's work. And if the abstract case cannot be made out, then the door is again opened to argue that specific philosophers should be held, or hold themselves, responsible for the harms they cause, just as any other member of a community would.

3. The Special Responsibilities of Philosophers

Having dispensed with the claim that philosophers should be seen as having diminished responsibilities toward the unintended political harms of their philosophizing, I wish now to consider arguments that would support a heightened political responsibility for philosophers. I will here be guided by parallel arguments advanced for heightened responsibilities of other professionals for the political and moral harms caused by their works. A key consideration in this discussion concerns the reasonable expectations that are created by the roles professional philosophers assume.

Philosophers have the professional duty to express their ideas in ways that minimize the likelihood of harm produced by their writings. Professionals are afforded special status in society, which generally includes a lack of vigilant public oversight of their work. All professionals have the positive duty to be especially vigilant in critically evaluating the possible harms that their work can cause. In this spirit, philosophers should view the texts that they compose in the critical light of the possible harms caused by their works. As I argued above, only when the dissemination of an idea is very important and the only way to disseminate it is to risk harm to others, is it possibly justified for philosophers to downplay the duty of due care concerning the consequences of their writings.

Consider again the case of Nietzsche. He clearly saw that the dissemination of his ideas was likely to cause harm due to misinterpretation. In a letter to Karl Knortz he said: "It is my deepest conviction that my problems, my whole 'immoralist' position, come much too soon for this age, which is still far too unprepared for them."[11] And yet Nietzsche felt that his ideas were so important, especially the ideas on "master morality," which he knew would fuel racist prejudice, that he felt he had to take the risk. On one occasion he had second thoughts and asked that the final part of *Thus Spake Zarathustra* be withdrawn from circulation because "It won't be ripe for publishing until after several decades of world-historical crises."[12] Nietzsche appears to have been aware of the possible harms of his writings, and yet he rarely tried to do anything to minimize these harms. Many other philosophers have simply ignored the possible harmful consequences of their writings, claiming that the importance of their ideas was sufficient justification for such disregard.

As we saw in chapter 5, professional responsibility is generally understood to involve a standard of due care, the disregard of which warrants the charge of professional negligence. Regardless of what a particular professional actually knows, that professional is expected to be aware of things that the members of the profession are reasonably expected to know. The standard of due care requires that members of a profession minimize harms resulting from the exercise of their professed knowledge, and the professional cannot use ignorance as an excuse. When specific members create harm unknowingly, even though they should be aware of the potentiality of these harms occurring, they risk the charge of professional negligence.

But what harms should philosophers be expected to be able to foresee or predict? Admittedly, it is very difficult to answer this question in an abstract way. Let me consider some relatively easy cases. Consider the case of Michael Levin, who clearly foresaw, but did not necessarily intend, that his writings about the supposed racial inferiority of Blacks in philosophy would offend Blacks and further perpetuate racial bias against Blacks.[13] Levin may not be blamable for the offense taken by those who read his works if the harm they experience is due to choices they themselves have made, or if the harm is both offset by and a necessary component of the value of Michael Levin's philosophizing. But the potential increase in racial bias is the kind of consequence that should not be disregarded.

If a philosopher's lack of foresight was based on inattention or ignorance, while others in the profession easily foresaw the harms resulting from the philosopher's action, then the resultant harms are among those the philosopher should have been expected to predict, and for which she or he should be responsible. Consider here the work of Rousseau on the general will, which inspired Robespierre. It seems reasonably clear that Robespierre abused Rousseau's notion of the general will in justifying the Reign of Terror. But it also seems clear that Rousseau should have foreseen that people might understand his idea in just this way, for there was a history of the political exploitation of similar ideas in France.[14] Again, while Rousseau may not be blamable for these harms, he is still at least partially responsible for them, since they are the sort of harm that Rousseau should have been able to predict.

I wish to stress again that I am addressing harms caused by philosophers that were foreseen or at least foreseeable. It would be quite unreasonable to suggest that Nietzsche should feel shame for harms produced by his writings due to some Rube Goldberg type of causal chain that resulted in harm many generations later. What I am proposing is that philosophers need to take more seriously than most currently do the *foreseeable* harmful consequences of their philosophy. In the clearcut cases, failure to take consequences seriously may result in the philosopher's partial responsibility for these consequences.

Beyond this point, we must rely on what it is *reasonable* to expect of people who are engaged in professional philosophical pursuits. In attempting to set out some parameters of professional vigilance against harm on the part of philosophers, let us consider what it would be important to know in order to be able to assess the potential consequences of one's philosophical writings. Obviously, one must first ascertain what the audience is likely to be. This would involve knowing about the distribution and marketing practices of one's publisher, as well as knowing, in general, where similar philosophy books have sold. In addition, one would need to know something about the political climate in those societies in which one's book is likely to be distributed and what reactions there have been to similar books. On this basis, one can begin to predict what the political consequences of one's writings might be. It would be fair to say that philosophers who fail to secure such information cannot claim ignorance as an excuse if their works cause harm.

Can a case be made for excusing from all political responsibility those who work in the more rarefied areas of philosophy, such as metaphysics, logic, or epistemology? My view is that metaphysicians, logicians, and epistemologists can no more relieve themselves of responsibility in this way than can poets or novelists or any other writers who do not explicitly take up political or moral themes. John Gardner argues that all art is subject to moral appraisal because it has the potential profoundly to influence its readers.[15] And while it is true that there are likely to be fewer political effects of writings in rarefied philosophical areas, it is also true that no area of philosophy is immune from exerting influence on its readers. And while it may seem that these influences are normally remote from political or moral matters, philosophers working in these rarefied fields should still exercise care when their writings are likely to have political or moral repercussions.

For this reason, philosophers normally cannot claim that their specialties are so far removed from political considerations as to relieve them of responsibility for certain easily foreseen political consequences of their writings. We may dismiss the objection, heard from those working in the more rarefied areas of philosophy, to my thesis concerning the special negative responsibility that philosophers have to minimize the harms that may result from the use or misuse of their philosophizing. When a philosopher decides to publish his or her work, that philosopher is already launched into the public arena, where the political and moral consequences of acts must be taken seriously. As I will argue in the next section of this paper, the very profession of philosophy is itself already a politicized domain. Before turning to this issue, I wish to offer a few caveats concerning what I have just set out.

In arguing for the heightened political responsibilities of philosophers, I wish to clarify my task in several ways. I am not urging that we blame a philosopher, qua philosopher, simply because his or her philosophizing leads to harms of a political sort. Rather, in the previous sections, I contended that philosophers cannot be relieved of responsibility for these harms merely by pointing to their professional status. In addition, I have just argued that in some cases philosophers need to exercise more care in the promulgation of their ideas than do most nonphilosophers. Disregard of this professional duty of philosophers may make them more responsible for resulting political harms than nonphilosophers would be.

If a philosophical work causes harm that would have been difficult to predict, the philosopher who wrote the work is normally not responsible at all for that harm. The one large class of exceptions to this rule concerns cases in which the content of a philosophy, once expressed, leads to clear harm during the philosopher's lifetime, but the philosopher in question does not distance his or her work from these harms. Of course, if it turns out, quite contrary to what the philosopher intended or should have foreseen, that the content of his or her philosophy, as reasonably interpreted, later causes harm, the philosophy may be indicted without implicating the philosopher.

In addition, the moral criticism of a philosopher's nonphilosophical activities does not necessarily implicate his or her philosophy. After all, we do not think better of a person's philosophy if it turns out that the person is a very good person, so there is no initial reason for thinking that philosophers who cause harm should have their philosophy impugned either. In this context one needs to ask whether the harmful acts of a philosopher were closely enough related to his or her philosophical beliefs. At present, there is quite a bit of controversy about whether Martin Heidegger's pro-Nazi actions really did, as he claimed, grow out of his metaphysics.[16] If they did, and I am not at present clear how this could be proven, then here would be a case in which a philosopher's harmful conduct illustrates why his or her philosophy should be impugned. But the exploration of this topic would take me far beyond the limits of the current chapter.

4. The Responsibilities of Philosophers as a Group

I turn finally to a consideration of the responsibilities of philosophers as a group to minimize political harms that might occur as a result of the practices of some of their members. As a group, philosophers constitute a profession that derives its high status from association with an illustrious short list of great philosophers in the history of the discipline. Just as the reputation of the group is enhanced by the great achievements of some of the group's members, so the reputation of the group should be diminished by the harms produced by some philosophers in certain societies. There is an important sense in which philosophers as a group are collectively responsible for what their members do, especially when the group achieves the status of an informal or formal association, as is true in most countries (including the American Philosophical Association in the United States), and to a more limited extent worldwide (as is true since the founding of the Federation Internationel des Societes de Philosophie). Such associations are able to exert control over their members by the use of various forms of sanctions, including expulsion from the group, brought against members who consistently violate the profession's norms.[17]

The profession of philosophers has the duty to seek to minimize the potential harms that its members could produce as members of the profession; for example, action might be needed if a member of the profession made racist remarks in the context of his or her professional role. There is diminished vigilance in public oversight of the profession, at least partly due to the appearance of internal oversight and control of the members by the professional association. In addition, philosophers as a group have the duty to speak out against the harmful use or misuse of philosophy. If professional philosophers as a group do not condemn such harms, they risk the public appearance of accepting such harms. Seeming to condone the harms would implicate the group in responsibility for them. Since the reputation of the group is created by public appearances, at least partially manipulated by professional philosophers as a group, any public appearance of support for members of the group who have caused harm should similarly be counted as a basis for the moral criticism of the group.[18]

Commenting on Martin Heidegger's public support of Nazism, Jurgen Habermas said that he felt compelled to condemn Heidegger, especially in light of Heidegger's refusal to renounce unambiguously his past acts of collaboration with the Nazis. In defending this assessment, Habermas said: "Insofar as we share a life-context and history with others, we have a right to call one another to account."[19] Insofar as philosophers, especially philosophers from the same society, share a common professional reputation and history, they may share in the harms of their fellow members if they do not speak out against the harmful practices.

Several years ago a debate raged among psychiatrists and psychologists about the practice in the Soviet Union of declaring political dissidents to be insane and hence psychologically unfit to live in society. This practice, which was supported by professional psychiatrists and psychologists in the Soviet Union, was ultimately condemned by several international psychological associations. The condemnation seems to have played a role in changing the policy. At the time, some members urged that their associations not take a public stand in order to avoid "politicizing" associations, which should remain above the fray of politics.[20] The argument that was advanced made reference to the necessarily nonpolitical nature of the professions in question. This argument is a variant of the argument by Rorty that I quoted earlier. I will close this chapter with a few additional remarks on this type of argument, especially when it is directed at the members of a profession considered as a group. Professions are necessarily public entities, and hence they are already not far removed from the political domain. While there may be some sense in claiming that individual psychologists or philosophers are outside the domain of politics, when these individuals seek to become members of a profession they make a public declaration about the kind of activity and expertise they profess. As I have indicated, this public professing is done for a specific purpose: to gain a special status in the society for the members of the group. From the moment that individuals unite themselves into a profession, it is no longer possible to claim that the group is nonpublic. Furthermore, insofar as the group attempts to lobby the members of society for scarce resources or relative status, the professional group "politicizes" itself. It is no longer legitimate for members of the group to argue that the group needs to beware of becoming politicized; in fact, for most professional groups, being politicized is the extant state of affairs.

It is for this reason that professional groups cannot appeal to their supposedly nonpolitical nature as a reason for failing to make public statements about the harmful practices of their members, or about the harmful uses or abuses of their members' works. As a result, professional philosophers, and other professionals, must confront directly the public and political duties they have resulting from the public status they have sought and now enjoy. Based on arguments provided in the previous chapter, it seems to me to be clear that once this public status is recognized, the group has the duty to attempt to minimize the harm that its members cause or that is caused by the use or misuse of their members' works. Failure to meet this duty implicates the group as a whole in the harms. And the group is implicated in ways that would not apply to other groups that have done all that can be reasonably expected to minimize such harms.

There are also other, more positive, political duties that philosophers have by virtue of being members of a professional group. Let me mention one positive political duty, as opposed to the negative duty to refrain from causing harm, which has been the main thrust of this chapter. Many philosophers have the duty to speak out on controversial political issues, since these philosophers have expertise in just the sort of argumentation that is relevant to such controversies. Philosophers are schooled in the resolution of especially difficult controversies, and they should apply those skills directly to aid their societies if it becomes appropriate to do so. The special, privileged position philosophers have been given in society, as I explained above, should make them feel that they have special responsibilities as well.[21]

In addition, the leaders of professional groups such as philosophical associations bear a special responsibility for harms resulting from endorsing, or appearing to endorse, various political movements or causes. Consider the remarks by Richard Rorty that I quoted at the beginning of this chapter. Given the context of the conference at which Rorty spoke, his remarks were interpreted as chastising politically active philosophers in the Third World, and by so doing attempting to change the practices of these philosophers toward a less politically responsible position. I have already indicated why I think that Rorty, as an individual philosopher, was wrong to do this. But in addition, as a leading member of his profession, Rorty created the appearance that U.S. philosophers took such a position. It is in this light that the philosophers who were quick to criticize Rorty aided the U.S. philosophical community by distancing that community from the acts of one of its leading members.

The status of being a leading member of a profession is so intimately connected with the status of the professional group that it is quite likely that endorsements by a leading member will be associated with the endorsements by the group itself. And such endorsements will obviously carry more weight among members of the public than endorsements made by people who are not leading members of well-respected professions. In professional life as in government, leaders have a special responsibility not to create the appearance of support for potentially harmful movements, unless they have very good evidence about the composition and intents of these movements. Heidegger's joining the Nazi party at a time when he was a leading philosopher in Germany, and when the harms likely to be perpetrated by the Nazi movement were clear, means that Heidegger should at least share in responsibility for the increased likelihood of harm produced by the endorsement of Nazism which his joining the Nazi party embodied.[22] And it is clear that other leading philosophers at that time needed quickly to condemn Heidegger's remarks so as not to implicate philosophy as a profession in Heidegger's complicity in the harms of the Nazis.

In Heidegger's defense, it might be claimed that he spoke out in favor of Nazism because he felt it was his positive duty to take a stand on this controversial movement, and it seemed to him that supporting Nazism was the right thing to do, not the thing that was likely to contribute to harm. Heidegger cannot be condemned for failing to see that he should have taken seriously the political effects he could bring about because of his position as one of the world's leading philosophers. Nonetheless, it seems clear that he incorrectly judged what those effects were likely to be. This is not the kind of mistake that relieves him of responsibility, for Heidegger should have been able to see that his actions would contribute further to the harms of Nazism. After all, several of his best students (Hannah Arendt and Hans Jonas, to name only two) had fled Germany rather than assume the academic positions for which Heidegger had trained them. Heidegger's actions tainted the reputation of philosophy, especially since they were not quickly condemned by other leading philosophers.

Throughout this chapter I have argued for the heightened political responsibilities of philosophers. In the first few sections of this chapter I argued that individual philosophers cannot sustain the argument that they have diminished political responsibilities by reference to the nature of their roles as gadflies and seekers of wisdom. I then argued that, indeed, philosophers, like various other professionals, have more political responsibilities concerning the effects of their writing and speaking than ordinary citizens do. And I ended by claiming that philosophers as a group also have the political responsibility to prevent the abuse of philosophy, especially if they are identified as key members of the profession. With the granting of special privileged status in society there must be connected special responsibilities. It is now time for philosophers to recognize the public price they must pay for the privileges they have successfully sought. In what follows I will address, in more general terms, the extent and limitations of a person's role responsibilities. Membership in a particular community is seen to be key both to the understanding of the pull of one's role responsibilities and to the limitations that must inevitably be placed on roles when they conflict.

[IGHT

Metaphysical Guilt and Moral Taint

In chapter 1, I suggested that existentialist views of responsibility have often been accused of being extreme and implausible. Existentialists argue, for instance, that membership in a group that causes great harm implicates all members of the group, even those who did not do anything to bring about the harm. Group membership, especially membership in a community, is held to carry with it increased moral responsibility. In this chapter, I wish to analyze the relationship between community membership and moral responsibility. I will defend a social existentialist account of a person's community-based responsibilities. In the final chapter I will indicate some of the limitations that should be placed on such a view.

It is true that existentialist views of responsibility expand greatly the normal realm of things (including attitudes, omissions, and even some effects over which one has no control) for which it is appropriate for a person to hold himself or herself responsible. But the view is not so extreme as it might first appear; being responsible is not the same as being morally guilty (which entails moral blameworthiness). Karl Jaspers made a major contribution to this debate when he suggested that there are types of guilt based on who one is and not on what one had done. The former type of guilt, which he calls "metaphysical guilt," does not necessarily translate into moral guilt, but it does entail some form of moral responsibility. In attempting to defend an existentialist account of responsibility I will defend the view, suggested several times in earlier chapters, that there are levels of being morally responsible, namely, those involving shame and moral taint, that are less severely accusatory than being morally guilty. Establishing these points will hopefully make more plausible the existentialist project of expanding the domain of responsibility.

In this chapter, I wish to investigate the legitimacy and status of responsibility attributions that concern what Jaspers calls "metaphysical guilt." In the first section, I will explore the concept of metaphysical guilt and attempt to identify the moral implications of attributions of metaphysical guilt. In the second section, I will attempt to link the experience of guilt, especially metaphysical guilt, with the notion of membership in a community. In the third section, I will examine cases in which communities contribute to major harms, but where the harm would occur even if a particular member made no contribution. By reference to the concept of metaphysical guilt, I contend that it does make sense to say that the members of some of these communities are morally tainted by, although not necessarily morally guilty for, these harms. In the fourth section, I will briefly take up the question of whether expanding the domain of responsibility to include metaphysical guilt, as existentialists have recommended, is advantageous.

1. The Concept of Metaphysical Guilt

In *The Question of German Guilt*, Karl Jaspers distinguishes moral from metaphysical guilt. The latter is defined as follows:

> There exists a solidarity among men as human beings that makes each co-responsible for every wrong and every injustice in the world, especially for crimes committed in his presence or with his knowledge. If I fail to do whatever I can to prevent them, I too am guilty. If I was present at the murder of others without risking my life to prevent it, I feel guilty in a way not adequately conceivable either legally, politically or morally. That I live after such a thing has happened weighs upon me as indelible guilt.[1]

There are two aspects of metaphysical guilt mentioned in this passage, which will form the basis of my expansion of Jaspers's important notion. As I will understand it in this chapter, metaphysical guilt arises out of each person's shared identity, out of the fact that people share membership in various groups that shape who these people are, and that each person is at least somewhat implicated in what any member of the group does. But metaphysical guilt is not merely based on group membership. Rather, it arises out of the fact that a person did not but could have (and should have) responded differently when faced with the harms committed by his of her fellow group members. The metaphysical guilt arises from the fact that one does nothing to prevent the harms, or at least to indicate disapproval of them. Due to these failures, the individual does nothing to disconnect himself or herself from those fellow group members who perpetrate harms. And while it may be that one is also *morally* guilty for one's omissions that contributed to the harm, what is important for *metaphysical* guilt is that one chose to do nothing to distance oneself from the harmful acts of one's fellow humans (or more plausibly, some smaller subgroup of humans). Metaphysical guilt is based not on a narrow construal of what one does, but rather on the wider concept of who one chooses to be.

There is an incomplete form of metaphysical guilt that existentialists have discussed. Sometimes metaphysical guilt is discussed as if it only concerned group membership, and not also the responses of an individual to the harms of his or her group. In the above quotation, Jaspers comes dangerously close to saying that each of us, merely by being members of the human race, share responsibility for all of the harms of the world. And Paul Ricoeur has discussed the concept of "original sin," in which everyone is guilty, "even little children in the wombs of their mothers."[2] Perhaps it is this occasional failure to recognize that metaphysical guilt has two aspects that is responsible for the view that existentialists hold to an implausible view of responsibility. Since I do not believe that the incomplete view is entailed by existentialist beliefs, nor is it a view widely accepted among existentialists, I will not address it in this chapter.[3]

Metaphysical guilt, even in its full and proper meaning, is clearly different from moral guilt. Jaspers illustrates this difference:

> There is no moral obligation to sacrifice one's life in the sure knowledge that nothing will have been gained. . . . But there is within us a guilt consciousness which springs from another source. . . . It is not enough that I cautiously risk my life to prevent it; if it happens, and if I was there, and if I survive where the other is killed, I know from a voice within myself: I am guilty of being still alive.[4]

One cannot move from the feeling of metaphysical guilt to any kind of claim about violating a moral obligation or duty. Being metaphysically guilty does not entail being morally guilty.

Yet Jaspers does believe that there is a kind of moral strand that is sometimes interwoven with metaphysical guilt:

And probably every German capable of understanding will transform his approach to the world and himself in the metaphysical experiences of such a disaster. How that will happen none can prescribe, and none antici- pate. It is a matter of individual solitude.[5]

In my social existentialist account, metaphysical guilt calls forth a certain kind of moral judgment. It forces upon the individual a reas- sessment of who he or she is. It calls for people to reflect upon and often change their attitudes and dispositions toward the harms of the world, even when it is impossible for these people to affect those harms now. And by changing one's stance toward the world, one changes oneself. Those who choose not to respond to the harms of their communities share moral responsibility, although not moral guilt, for these harms. I believe that shame or taint are the moral con- cepts most closely connected to metaphysical guilt. To avoid moral shame or taint, people must change who they are in the face of their communities' harms.

Sartre discusses these issues in some detail under the subject of "authenticity." In *Anti-Semite and Jew,* Sartre defines "authenticity" as follows:

> Authenticity, it is almost needless to say, consists in hav- ing a true and lucid consciousness of the situation, in as- suming the responsibilities and risks that it involves, in accepting it in pride or humiliation, sometimes in horror and hate.
>
> There is no doubt that authenticity demands much courage, and more than courage.[6]

Authenticity involves, among other things, being conscious of who one is and taking responsibility for the harms of one's class, one's position, and one's situation in the world. To be "inauthentic" is to "deny" or "attempt to escape from" one's condition, to fail to as- sume responsibility for choosing to be who one is.[7]

Authenticity concerns a kind of responsibility that is neither polit- ical nor narrowly moral, if we think of morality as referring to the realm of explicit behavior. But since choice is involved, there is a moral dimension nonetheless. As Sartre says, "The choice of au- thenticity appears to be a *moral* decision . . . but in no way serving as a solution on the social or political level."[8] Indeed, the authentic person is not necessarily one who changes his or her explicit be- havior in light of moral norms. Rather, the authentic person often lacks the ability to change his or her explicit behavior at all; Sisyphus lacked the ability to stop climbing, even though he did have the ability to control how he reacted mentally to his fate.

Nonetheless, for Sartre there is a moral dimension to authenticity; this is my own view as well. Sartre devotes a lot of attention to the authentically appropriate kinds of attitudinal response a person should make concerning the life situations he or she faces. It matters whether one accepts one's situation with pride or humiliation, with horror or hate, Sartre tells us. These attitudes and dispositions are, of course, not merely emotional responses to one's situation. Rather, they are clearly meant to be arrived at reflectively. But most importantly, as I will argue, the appropriateness of these dispositions and attitudes is a moral appropriateness. Even when we cannot change the world with our actions, we can make other choices, "original choices," concerning what Thomas Flynn calls the "criteria according to which we deliberate and decide" as to how we approach our world.[9]

As I construe it, metaphysical guilt only entails *moral* responsibility, if by "moral responsibility" we mean responsibility for attitudes and character traits as well as for behavior. Inauthenticity involves a failure to see oneself as accountable for who one is; this is surely a failure of character, indeed a type of cowardice. The authentic person has the virtue of courage and as a result meets head-on his or her faults as well as the faults of fellow community members, regarding himself or herself as at least partially responsible for them. The inauthentic person is metaphysically guilty, but given that being inauthentic does not involve simple choices of how to behave, moral guilt is often inappropriate.

The underlying principle of existentialist ethics is that one is always morally *responsible* for who one chooses to be, that is, for choices of attitude, disposition, and character, as well as for one's behavior. One needs to become consciously aware of who one is, as a necessary, although not sufficient, step toward reflectively understanding one's life and then deciding whether to change it. The discussion of authenticity for Sartre, and of metaphysical guilt for Jaspers, reveals that people should strive to understand who they are and to approach the self with a strong enough attitude of accountability to take necessary steps to change themselves for the better whenever possible. Here it is vitally important that people regard themselves as accountable for their metaphysical states, even when they cannot do that which would change these states.

Authenticity involves a deep feeling of accountability for one's self. Not everyone who is inauthentic or metaphysically guilty is also morally guilty, because not everyone can change his or her self or situation. As Jaspers points out, people are not morally guilty for failing to do those things that have very little likelihood of changing anything. But people are morally responsible for becoming consciously aware of their situations, for only when they are so aware will it be possible to change for the better when change becomes possible. In Sartre's own words:

> If someone gives me this world with its injustices, it is not so that I may coolly contemplate them but so that I may animate them by my indignation, expose them and show their nature as injustices, that is, as abuses to be suppressed.[10]

Of course, being indignant in the face of the injustices perpetrated by one's community does not necessarily lead to an overcoming of those injustices. In normal circumstances, people should do more than merely express indignation. What Sartre is getting at is that no matter how restricted one's options are, one still has the choice of the attitude one takes toward the injustices of the world. The choice of whether or not to be indignant is something that occurs deep in the psyche and is almost always a choice that is open to us. If we merely passively accept injustices, then we choose to align ourselves with them. This is what makes us both metaphysically guilty and morally responsible, although not necessarily morally guilty, for these injustices.

There is an important collective dimension to metaphysical guilt. It is important, morally speaking, that certain evils or harms occur through facilitation by one's group, even in cases in which there is nothing that the group's members could have done, on their own or even in combination with others, except in the very long run, to prevent these evils or harms. The group solidarity that Jaspers identifies as one of the key ingredients in metaphysical guilt creates a moral taint for all of those members whose group is in any way implicated in evils or harms. To use Jaspers's own example, it is appropriate that all Germans feel tainted by what their fellow Germans did, and such a feeling should persist even for the many people who could have done nothing differently, in terms of individual or collective behavior, to prevent Hitler's reign of terror. In the next section I will attempt to answer the question: What is it about the fact that one is a *member* of a group that is causally responsible for a major harm that morally taints the members?

2. Guilt and Community Membership

An existentialist account of responsibility can be rendered initially plausible by noting that people often feel pride, as well as shame or guilt, for what their fellow community members have done. The sheer fact of one's membership in a biologically or geographically defined group is normally not under one's control. But what is under one's control, and hence the subject of appropriate feelings of responsibility, is how one positions oneself in terms of that group. In communities, as in other groups, it is not mere membership that creates responsibility, but how one reacts (behaviorally or attitudinally) to the groups of which one is a member. In this section, I will mainly try to explain why people have feelings of responsibility based on group membership. I leave the question of the appropriateness of such feelings to the next section.

It is undeniable that being a member of a particular community that participates in harmful activity often causes some kind of moral feeling of guilt or taint for some members of the community, even though the individuals who feel guilt could not have prevented the harm from occurring. I am thinking of such examples as Americans feeling guilt for My Lai and Germans feeling guilt for the Holocaust. We are here still in the domain of metaphysical guilt, but focusing on the lack of effective choices at the community level. And we are now forced to think about moral responsibility in terms that are quite different from the normal model of moral guilt. For if there really was nothing an individual member of a community could have done to prevent the community from participating in a harm, and the individual did not, on his or her own, actually aid his or her community in this participation, moral responsibility, at least understood on the model of individual moral guilt, would be inappropriate.

Racism, so psychological studies claim, is a function of the socialization, as well as other forms of social interaction, that occurs within groups.[11] Yet it is common for people to say that they feel guilt for such things as the racial violence perpetrated by fellow community members where racist attitudes are commonplace. Merely by sharing common attitudes, why is it that some members of groups feel a sense of shared responsibility for what some other members do as a result of having these attitudes? An attitude, of course, is not the sort of thing about which people reach agreement. Indeed, an attitude, especially a group attitude, is not even an undertaking, in the sense that it is not consciously arrived at. But the feeling of moral responsibility may still be linked to one's choices. For people make choices about how to regard, or respond to, the dominant attitudes in their communities, and even how to react to the attitudes they themselves have been initially socialized to form by their communities. Such reactions form the basis for possible changes in who one is. Thus, such guilt feelings do not involve the incomplete view of metaphysical guilt mentioned above. For the people who feel guilty in these cases made choices concerning how to react to their own and others' attitudes within the community where harms occurred.

Consider the case of racism in a group such as a university community. Of course, most universities have a central decision-making structure, but I will use the term "university community" to stand for the less formally structured group of students, teachers, and staff who are connected, in widely diverse ways, to the central administration. What all the members of such a community share is a culture: a set of intellectual, aesthetic, and social influences continuing over time. Cultures bind the members of a group together by providing common experiences and viewpoints, thus perpetuating a form of solidarity that Jaspers spoke of. The intense interaction of ideas means that the members of a group in which there is a shared culture identify themselves with the group and in a sense with one another. Of course, the identification may be very weak, especially for members who are only on the fringe of the community; and in such cases the group identification may be so weak as not to generate feelings of metaphysical guilt. But I am mainly interested in the experiences of those who do feel such guilt.

When a group develops a culture, then that group is not merely an aggregate; like a decision-making procedure, a culture allows for the amalgamation of individual actions and attitudes into something more than the mere sum of its parts. Most importantly, cultures are both the products of individual actions and attitudes and the producers of new actions and attitudes in the world. Attitudes that arise within a culture are often very different from attitudes that arise among individuals who do not share a common culture. A cross-fertilization of ideas occurs when members of the group react to the views of fellow members who are perceived as like-minded.

The shared attitudes within a community come, over time, to

create a shared identification, a shared feeling of solidarity. Just as the members of a community gain a personal sense of pride from the accomplishments of the community as a whole, as well as from the accomplishments of their fellow members, so the members of a community often come to feel shame or moral taint for harms members of their community have caused. People in communities share more than a sense of the accomplishments within the group; they also share a sense of the failures. This is what generates the sense of responsibility that members of a community feel for the harms that their communities participate in.

The solidarity of a community often creates a shared feeling of responsibility for what occurs within the group. This feeling of responsibility is linked to that part of one's identity that is based on the groups of which one is a member. It is not merely that one is a member of a group within which harmful attitudes, for instance, have become dominant. Sometimes feeling responsible is based on the sense that something wrong was done by one's group members, which one also could easily have done. Sometimes there is the feeling that one should have done something to break the chain linking one, as a nonoffending party, to the rest of the group. Of course, a person could not cease to be ethnically German, but he or she could have disavowed or condemned what other Germans believed or were currently doing. Such acts of language or mind may break the chain of responsibility between individual and community. Condemning or disavowing what one's community has done changes the part of one's self that is based on how one chooses to regard oneself. Such changes disassociate one from fellow group members and diminish one's shared responsibility for what those others have done.

As I said above, the existentialist view is sometimes interpreted as holding that even when one has distanced oneself from one's group, there should still be a feeling of moral responsibility for what the group does. The most plausible explanation of this shared responsibility is that solidarity continues to make one identify with what the group does, regardless of whether one has tried to distance oneself from the acts of the group. I think that this more extreme version of metaphysical guilt is only partially justifiable. As an actual account of why it is that some people feel guilt in such cases, it is worth attention and seems to contain a germ of truth. But as an account of one's *appropriate* feelings, the account should not be accepted. Jaspers seems to recognize this point when he distinguishes between guilt associated with merely being a member of a group versus guilt associated with condoning what the group has done.[12]

The examples we have considered so far illustrate the metaphysical guilt resulting from membership in, and acceptance of, a certain group that has caused harm. The guilt is metaphysical because it has to do with who one chooses to be, in the sense of acceptance or rejection of such an affiliation, rather than what one has actually done. But what is the appropriate moral feeling connected with metaphysical guilt? Moral guilt is appropriate when there is something that a person brought about in the world. Being a causal agent is closely connected to moral guilt. But when a person's causal agency is not in question, or at least when the causal role one played did not make a difference in the world, then moral shame or taint may be the appropriate moral feeling. We are thrust into the domain of responsibility for who one is, and the terms of judgment should be different from those addressed to a person's explicit behavior. I explore this point further by turning next to the difficult case of an individual who feels tainted by being a member of a community that has participated in harm, when there was nothing the individual could have done to prevent the harm. A consideration of this case will allow us to examine what reasons can be advanced for thinking that there are appropriate moral feelings that correspond with metaphysical guilt.

3. The Case of South African Divestment

Consider the case of university investments in companies that support apartheid in South Africa. Anthony Appiah has raised this question: What if, contrary to fact, the divestment of a university's shares of stock in companies doing business with South Africa would make no difference in the world? Assume that some different university or other buyer would purchase the shares of stock of which a given university divests itself. Appiah argues that it is a mistake to think that moral responsibility should be assigned to the members of this community, even though some feel tainted by what their community has done.[13] In what follows I will set out Appiah's reasons for holding this view, and then I will challenge his conclusions from the standpoint of an existentialist understanding of metaphysical guilt.

Appiah begins by claiming that there is a difference between ancient and modern conceptions of morality. "For us [moderns]," he says, "what matters is not who you are but what you try to do." Taint is a category left over from ancient times, when people's responsibility was determined by group affiliation. Appiah is generally skeptical of the older tradition, especially because "people may be stigmatized for their unintended association with evil." And, says Appiah, such a person may be tainted or polluted "by that association even though he or she took all the care in the world to avoid it."[14] The ancient conceptions of morality did not properly distinguish behavior from character. Yet, according to Appiah, character is often a function of factors, like group membership, over which people do not have control. Appiah claims that it is simply anachronistic for people today to rely on this ancient conception.

Appiah's characterization of the ancient concept of taint or pollution is only partially correct. In the most famous treatment of the development of Greek values, Arthur Adkins distinguishes between a Homeric and a post-Homeric conception of taint or pollution. For Homeric Greeks, pollution is "the presence (or supposed presence) of any substance, of whatever kind, which is believed to hamper men's relations with the supernatural. . . . But there is nothing metaphysical about this 'pollution'. It is dirt, real physical dirt, which must be removed before a man may pray to the gods, with any expectation that they will listen to him."[15]

In post-Homeric Greece, Adkins argues, pollution has a decidedly metaphysical dimension, much akin to a sense of guilt, although not moral guilt. Someone who is polluted, because, say, his brother committed murder, is not considered to be immoral. Pollution is here largely a nonmoral phenomenon, although "its influence is felt strongly in certain moral contexts."[16] As in existential conceptions of inauthenticity and metaphysical guilt, in the post-Homeric conception of pollution metaphysical and moral guilt are clearly separated. Appiah may be correct in claiming that a person could be tainted even though that person took all the care in the world; but *moral* assessment of this person is not unaffected by the care that the person took to avoid associating with evil, or by how the person subsequently reacted to that association.

Adkins persuasively argues that even though all those who killed were polluted, post-Homeric Athenian law distinguished between types of homicide, even including the category "*phonos dikaios,* homicide for which the law prescribed no penalty."[17] If the pollution one brought upon oneself by one's own acts could be mitigated legally and morally, so could the pollution caused by associating with the evil acts of others. So Appiah is right to think that ancient people believed that a person could not escape from "metaphysical stain" when they associated with evil; but at least some ancient people believed that a person could affect the moral assessment attached to that metaphysical stain.

There is another sense of taint, Appiah tells us, which is distinctively modern but which is not necessarily something we should endorse either. Modern taint is assigned on the basis of a kind of "dirty hands." Appiah asks us to consider the case of those who are members of a university community that owns stock in a company that "provides equipment which the South African government uses to maintain the system of apartheid." In such cases, we, the members, "are associated, through our ownership of the shares with a wicked system; we play a part in it. Our holding of the shares taints us."[18] All that any of us, individually or collectively, can do is to disassociate ourselves from apartheid, but we cannot change it. Here we do engage in a type of behavior; if we are tainted, it is not merely on the basis of who we are. But, while our behavior links us to an evil, Appiah assumes, contrary to fact, that there is no change in behavior on our part that will mitigate the evil. If these are the facts, then, according to Appiah, the existence of the evil is not something under our control, and hence it is also not something for which we are morally responsible, even if we feel tainted by it.

In the pure case Appiah asks us to imagine, apartheid will not be diminished by our acts. Appiah sets out these features of the case that concern us:

1. The act we are contemplating is intended to remove us from a certain relation to a series of acts which is morally deplorable.
2. We are profiting from this relation; although we could make nearly the same profit without this relationship to apartheid.
3. Nevertheless, the act we are contemplating (working to achieve divestment) will make no difference to the evil of apartheid; except that people other than ourselves will then profit from this relationship.[19]

Even though we feel tainted by our university's continuing participation in the evil of apartheid, it is not appropriate that we hold ourselves morally responsible for this evil, in Appiah's view.

Appiah says that it is important for our sense of moral integrity that our actions not taint us with evil, but he does not think that this is relevant for moral responsibility. Appiah thinks that it might be important for people to maintain their sense of integrity, even when the changes in behavior necessary for maintaining integrity make no other difference in the world. For integrity makes a difference for the agent, and of course this is a difference in the world. If people did not have a sense of integrity, and did not act on that sense, their lives would surely be the worse for it. But this is the only basis that Appiah finds for thinking that these considerations should have any moral sway on our behavior.

There is much more to be said in support of the moral importance of taint than is captured in Appiah's few lines on the value of integrity. Appiah is wrong initially to think that what a person does or tries to do is unrelated to who that person is. Indeed, even if who one is has to do with group affiliations, one is almost always in a position to denounce or condemn one's group. The influence exerted by groups on one's identity is diminished by one's ability to choose which groups one joins, as well as by how one reacts to the groups one finds oneself in. Insofar as it is possible to distance oneself from one's group affiliations, one is able to exert significant influence on one's metaphysical self in ways that have moral importance. Those individuals who can, but choose not to, distance themselves from groups that are contributing to harm are metaphysically guilty and also morally responsible for, in the sense of being morally tainted by, the harms caused by their fellow group members or institutions. For those who cannot distance themselves, their taint need not have any moral implications.

There are three notions of taint that can be associated with metaphysical guilt. The most common form, which is closely akin to guilt by association, is based on one's associations, regardless of whether one is even aware of having such associations. For example, merely being Jewish might be said to make one tainted by the actions of Jews in another part of the world, about whom one knows nothing. Obviously, in this group of cases one's association with evil does not have anything to do with what one chooses to do and should not normally have much to do with one's moral responsibilities. But the two other kinds of taint, those based on associations one could distance oneself from and those based on associations one could end, but which, if ended, would still not make any difference in the world, are much more important morally than Appiah would lead us to believe. For in both cases, it matters that one could cut the link between oneself and these groups and thereby affect one's moral identity.

From my social existentialist viewpoint, in order to avoid the responsibility associated with taint it is necessary to take reasonable steps to distance oneself from the harm caused by one's group. What counts as "reasonable steps" will vary according to context. In the case of South African apartheid, it is clear that one should do more than merely disapprove of one's university for not divesting. But it is unclear to me whether one needs to march on the president's office in order fully to avoid sharing in responsibility for the harms of apartheid. The question that each person needs to ask is: Have I done all that can reasonably be expected of me to distance myself from this harm?

Consider the case we spoke about in section 1, of Germans feeling guilty for atrocities perpetrated by fellow Germans against Jews in the 1930s and 1940s. What matters is that these people were associated, through membership in the German nationality, with those who perpetrated the atrocities. It does not matter whether or not there was anything that most Germans could have done personally to change the outcome. We should not engage in guilt by association. But in the German case, some people were aware of what was happening and could, by the ability that all people had, denounce or at least disavow the atrocities, and thereby distance themselves from the harm. Given this ability, then at least some of the taint an individual German felt, perhaps all that it was appropriate to feel, remained connected both to what he or she tried (or failed to try) to do and to who he or she was. And in these cases taint is appropriately seen as a form of moral responsibility for who one has chosen to be. Taint is not merely to be avoided because it disrupts the integrity of the self.

In Appiah's pure case of divestment in South African companies, the same result can be reached as in the case of German guilt. One almost always has the existential option to disavow the associations one finds oneself in. Therefore, Appiah is wrong to think that in his case there is a great divide between who one is and what one tries to do. These are related notions, just as there is a relationship between certain metaphysical states and an individual's moral responsibility. It is worth noting once again that I do not mean to suggest that one is *morally guilty* for these states, since metaphysical guilt does not entail moral guilt. Appiah is right to think that taint, rather than moral guilt, really is the right concept in the cases we have been considering. But Appiah is wrong to think that theories of moral responsibility should not have a place for taint. In the final section of this chapter, I will conclude with a brief discussion of the importance of moral taint in a conception of moral responsibility.

4. Expanding the Domain of Moral Responsibility

One of the most obvious objections to the views I have here articulated is that I have expanded the notion of moral responsibility too far; it no longer has the motivational force it had when it was restricted to behavior for which a person could be said to be morally guilty. Thomas Jefferson once referred to this sort of concern as the fear of "incessant responsibility."[20] This objection perhaps has its greatest poignancy with respect to the discussion of moral taint. According to this characterization, the concept of taint is thought to play a useful role only in that it marks out the field of the nonobligatory but nonetheless ideally virtuous life. In an ideal world we would like not to be associated in any way at all with the perpetuation of harm or evil. We are tainted by these associations, and we regret them, but, so the objection goes, that should be all. We should not think that we have failed in our moral responsibilities. I wish to challenge this view in these last brief remarks.

For virtually every person, individual identity is intimately connected with group membership. From a moral perspective, it is vitally important that people continue to feel motivated to shape and reshape their communities and other groups. When the members of a university community resign themselves to their university's involvement in apartheid, they also resign themselves to association with moral evil, and they thereby resign themselves to having their identities shaped in ways they would not choose. Given the importance of communities in shaping a person's moral character, significant options for moral and social change are cut off as soon as the individual feels overwhelmingly determined by group affiliations.

Let us recall Sartre's remarks about being responsible for being born.[21] We do not choose to be born, in the sense of being able to influence the time, place, and circumstances of our birth, but there are choices we make concerning our birth that affect our responsibility. Sartre's position has some plausibility, in that we do have an "originary choice" about at least some of the facts of our birth. We can resign ourselves to the facts of our birth or we can rebel against them, at least in terms of the attitudes we take toward them. We may be born into a group that has a history of terrorizing minorities, and we may have no opportunity to change the group's behavior, but we can affect the way the group affiliation shapes our selves. While we cannot deny that we are, say, U.S. citizens by birth, we can strongly condemn what the United States has done in a particular case and thereby reshape our selves (and perhaps also reshape what it means for others to consider themselves U.S. citizens).

The existentialist project cannot seriously be slighted for not being important. But it can be slighted for widening our concepts of moral responsibility to such an extent that people no longer feel as strongly motivated to avoid harm as they once did, when responsibility was tightly connected only to guilt. Moral taint is certainly not as severe a condemnatory moral category as is moral guilt. And this is as it should be. People must feel motivated to avoid directly causing harm to others. But this motivation is not necessarily weakened by including other "lesser crimes" in the list of things for which people should feel a sense of moral responsibility. People continue to feel strongly motivated to avoid committing murder, even though there are other, lesser laws, such as traffic laws, that they are legally obligated not to violate.

Even if our sense of motivation to avoid "capital" moral crimes would be lessened by the introduction of "lesser" moral crimes, there are clearly important offsetting advantages to stressing the avoidance of moral taint. Again, it is necessary to think about the relationship between responsibilities and communities. By feeling motivated to avoid the taint of community-associated harm, people will see their moral responsibilities as calling for involvement in what their fellow community members are doing. Of course, this does not mean that people should invade one another's privacy or seek to curtail one another's "harmless immoralities." Rather, I am only addressing the kind of harm to others that disrupts communal harmony and is contrary to the common good. (The next chapter is devoted, in part, to explicating and delimiting this kind of harm.) Moral taint is a concept that emphasizes that people should feel responsible when their fellow community members engage in these harms.

As I claimed in the discussion of collective inaction in chapter 6, seeing one's own moral status as interrelated with that of one's fellow group members will negate the tendency to ignore the most serious moral evils, those which can only be thwarted by the collective efforts of communities. The social existentialist emphasis on the moral importance of metaphysical guilt takes seriously our group affiliations and thereby sets the stage for taking seriously our shared responsibility for the great tragedies our communities have perpetrated. In the next chapter I will address some of the limitations that should be placed on responsibility when it is linked to the roles we play, or could play, in our communities.

NINE

Role Conflicts, Community, and Shared Agency

Social roles generally increase the domain of responsibility for those who assume or who agree to be cast into these roles. But a person's responsibilities may conflict, requiring some limits to be placed on their further expansion. The problem confronted in this chapter is that appeals to role responsibilities have often been made to attempt to limit a person's potential for effecting social change. If the account of shared responsibility I have developed is to avoid this pitfall, some basis for limiting role responsibilities must be identified. In this chapter I will explain both the pull of our role responsibilities and the limitations on them, limitations based on the sense of shared agency I discussed in chapter 2.

In the first section of this chapter, I look at the notion of a social role, attempting to explain why roles increase our moral responsibilities. I also attempt to explain why it is that conflicts of responsibility arise within a community. In the second section I sketch a pluralistic, social existentialist basis for adjudicating conflicts of responsibility. In the third section I return to the concept of shared agency to help understand the community involvement that is called for by shared membership. Here I rebut charges made by postmodernists that attempts such as mine, which rely on concepts of shared agency, deny differences among peoples. Finally, I will discuss several proposals similar to mine, which have recently been made by philosophers concerned about shared agency. I will explain why several of these proposals support discriminatory social traditions by following the conservative communitarian doctrine that makes social role an overriding moral concept, and I will contrast this view with a liberationist communitarianism.

1. Roles and Conscientiousness

Sartre provides us with an excellent example of a conflict of role responsibilities. In his controversial essay "Existentialism is a Humanism," Sartre describes the case presented to him by one of his pupils:

> His father was quarrelling with his mother and was also inclined to be a "collaborator"; his elder brother had been killed in the German offensive of 1940 and this young man, with a sentiment somewhat primitive but generous, burned to avenge him. His mother was living alone with him, deeply afflicted by the semi-treason of his father and by the death of her eldest son, and her one consolation was in this young man. But he, at this moment, had the choice between going to England to join the Free French Forces or of staying near his mother and helping her live.[1]

Here is a classic case of the conflicting responsibilities of a child to his parent and of a citizen to his homeland. Existentialists, such as Sartre, generally do not believe that there are algorithms that will allow us to adjudicate such conflicts. But the radical view of responsibility that existentialists espouse is not insensitive to the problem of such conflicts and to the need to address such conflicts in an account of the expanded domain of responsibility. In this section I will attempt to develop a social existentialist response to the problem of role-responsibility conflicts.

Role responsibilities are responsibilities one has by virtue of having agreed to take on a certain set of tasks in society, or perhaps by virtue of having agreed to be thrust into the position of assuming various tasks. The key element here is that one voluntarily chooses or agrees to undertake various duties one would not normally have. The individual who is drafted may not have voluntarily chosen to become a soldier, but this person must have voluntarily consented to the system of government that authorized his or her induction into the army for this person morally to have assumed the duties of being a soldier. If there is not such a voluntary affirmation, then the supposed duties are not morally compelling. The voluntary choice of the position and of the duties entailed by taking the position commit a person to the duties and make them his or her responsibility.

H. L. A. Hart makes a very interesting point about the concept of role responsibility. Not all of one's social duties are things for which one is morally responsible. Hart contrasts the case of a soldier who is detailed "to keep the camp clean and tidy for the general's visit of inspection" and the case of a soldier who is "merely told to remove a piece of paper from the approaching general's path." The former task is something that the soldier has "as his sphere of responsibility" involving "care and attention over a protracted period of time," since these duties are of a "relatively complex or extensive kind." The latter task is "at most his [social] duty," but not something for which the soldier is morally responsible.[2]

Moral responsibility attaches to social roles only if the people serving in the roles have a certain amount of autonomy over the choice and content of those roles. Existentialists would urge that we expand the domain of those things over which people are understood to have control (so as to include certain attitudes and omissions, as well as some roles). But generally, I believe, existentialists would support the point that Hart is making. Certain roles that a person has been thrust into and that the person has not consented to (for instance, traditional gender roles) should not be regarded as things the neglect of which we are morally responsible for.

In chapters 5 and 7 we discussed the legitimate expectations people have of professionals. Professional responsibility, a subset of role responsibility, is assigned to those who profess to have certain knowledge or skill that sets them apart from the other members of a community. The roles professionals assume create privileges for the professionals, and their increased responsibilities are linked to their privileged status in the society. A profession is different from an isolated task, in that a profession carries with it a set of duties concerning a relatively autonomous field of activity and lasting over the course of one's professional life, as a sort of cost of having professional privileges; in contrast, the roles associated with discrete tasks are generally not things that define a realm of autonomous behavior for a lifetime.

Role responsibility makes the most sense in the context of a relatively autonomous field of action (perhaps what leads Hart to talk about a sphere of responsibility, or better, a sphere of decision-making control). Employees have the social duty to follow the legitimate orders of their superiors, but unless these orders are intimately connected with the employees' freely assumed roles, it will be a mistake to say that they have a *moral* responsibility to meet these social duties. Drawing this distinction will help, in some cases, to adjudicate between conflicts of responsibility.

It is also important to be able to distinguish roles that carry duties to everyone and are hence universal in scope, from roles that have special obligations attached to them, in that they are owed on the basis of particular relationships people have entered into. Roles calling for people to show favoritism to those with whom they are in special relationships will often conflict with general obligations and responsibilities to avoid harm. As we have discussed, doctors and lawyers are thought to have special responsibilities, which sometimes override the general duty to tell the truth or to avoid all forms of harm in their communities.

Conflicts of responsibility are worsened by the fact that it is thought to be a virtue for a person to pursue his or her roles conscientiously. Conscientiousness is the single-minded pursuit of what one believes to be right or good. In ordinary speech, the term is most often associated with individual conduct within the context of a social role; for example, "He is a conscientious father," "She is a conscientious teacher." The term is also used, less commonly, to refer to a person in general. A "conscientious person" is either someone who carries out his or her tasks with scrupulous attention to what each task requires, or someone who more generally follows the dictates of his or her conscience in reaching decisions about how to conduct his or her affairs.

In Sartre's case we have a person who has chosen, or at least agreed, to assume the social role of caretaking son, which in this case involves the subjugation of personal happiness and even personal preferences to the needs and preferences of another person, that is, a demanding aged parent. For some people it might appear that the conscientious way to fulfill such a role is not just to conform to the standards of the role, but to become obsequious, fawning, and even slavish in carrying out the tasks associated with the role. A person described as being servile may merely be a person who conscientiously fulfills a social role that calls for service to the needs of another person.

The role of housewife has been understood in many cultures to entail devotion to family, especially to one's husband. A woman who pursues this role with single-minded devotion will always choose to place the interests of her spouse and family above her own interests. In attempting to serve her husband, she may become servile, as the greatest sign of personal devotion to her spouse. Indeed, such a person may cease to be a good citizen or neighbor so as to be even better at heeding her husband's beck and call. Such conscientious devotion to a specific social role can clearly conflict with a person's more general moral responsibilities, perhaps as citizen or neighbor.

The conscience of a person who has chosen to assume, or agreed to be cast into, a social role will sometimes appear to motivate that person to perform scrupulously the tasks associated with the role. Perhaps this is a reason why some people would be more strongly inclined to stay with an aged mother rather than to join the Free French Forces. As the tasks associated with a role become diffuse, or as the people to whom one owes the duties attached to the role become numerous, it is harder to be single-minded in pursuing one's role. Conscience often seems to demand that we take our role responsibilities quite seriously. When conflicts of responsibility arise, conscience seems to push us toward those roles that are relatively easy to fulfill, such as our specific role responsibilities, and into which we can throw ourselves, rather than toward our more general responsibilities to prevent harm or to be a good citizen.

Sartre argues that such solutions, based on what feels best at the time, are too simple; the justifications for them, which are based on what seems easiest at the time, involve a circularity of reasoning. He writes:

> If values are uncertain, if they are still too abstract to determine the particular, concrete case under consideration, nothing remains but to trust our instincts. That was what the young man tried to do; and when I saw him he said "In the end, it is feeling that counts, the direction in which it is really pushing me is the one I ought to choose. If I feel I love my mother enough to sacrifice everything else for her—my will to be avenged, all my longings for action and adventure—then I stay with her." . . . The value of his feeling for his mother was determined precisely by the fact that he was standing by her. . . . I can only estimate the strength of his affection if I have performed an action by which it is defined and ratified. But if I then appeal to this affection to justify my action, I find myself drawn into a vicious circle.[3]

The citizen, as well as the son, has specific moral responsibilities resulting from voluntary acts. And the standpoint of conscience, from which one tries to adjudicate conflicts of responsibility, does not clearly point us toward that responsibility supported by the stronger feeling. Indeed, conscience itself is grounded on two often conflicting bases, natural sentiments and reasonableness.

2. Conflicts of Responsibility

In this section I wish to develop some rules of thumb, which will allow us to begin to adjudicate some of the seemingly more intractable conflicts of responsibility. Such rules of thumb will be closely tied to the concept of the common good, which forms the centerpiece for any understanding of the value of both community and individual. I will begin with a few more remarks on the nature of conscience and then turn to the kind of restrictions needed if conscience is to be a good adjudicator of conflicts of responsibility. These restrictions are drawn in terms of "reasonableness," in that they attempt to offset the kind of problem that results when one's single-minded pursuit of a particular good blinds one to the common good.

Conscience, like virtue, is a capacity that often leads to socially beneficial consequences in those who develop it. As Philippa Foot has claimed, virtues are "corrective, each one standing at a point at which there is some temptation to be resisted or deficiency of motivation to be made good."[4] Similarly, conscience places barriers in one's path, which contribute to the avoidance of wrongdoing. Yet conscience, unlike virtue, seems to be grounded in a concern for the self, for the self's inner harmony, rather than directed toward the common good. While it is quite likely that Foot is right in claiming that there is no general virtue of self-love, conscience does seem to be different from virtue, in that it proceeds from and remains closely allied to a conception of what is of value to the self.

Conscientious behavior is behavior based on the realization or judgment that doing certain acts would violate the inner harmony or integrity of the self. But in certain circumstances regard for the integrity of the self promotes a particularly helpful regard for the welfare of other selves. Specifically, conscience can lead a person to see that a respect for internal harmony leads to a respect for harmony in general. And respect for harmony leads one to see that respect for a plurality of interests in a community is the key to conflict adjudication. I will try to lay the groundwork for such a conception by considering some of the things Hannah Arendt says about the experience of conscience.

Hannah Arendt, to my way of thinking a paradigmatic social existentialist, provides some good insights here by expanding on remarks made by Socrates. Arendt claims that moral judgment and aesthetic or political judgment are very similar.[5] In aesthetic judgment one can judge whether a particular painting is beautiful or ugly, even though one is unable to give general criteria of beautifulness. We often characterize this as an intuitive judgment. Arendt, following Kant, describes this intuition by saying that we place ourselves in an enlarged mentality when we make such judgments, that is, we anticipate the communication we would have with others and we predict the aesthetic judgments those others would make, and then we try to come to some sort of consensus between those others and ourselves. Similarly, in some moral judgments one judges that a particular act is wrong, yet one generally cannot give criteria of goodness or rightness. Again this seems to be an intuitive judgment in which we base the judgment on the anticipated communication we would have between ourselves and other selves.

Arendt builds on insights gleaned from Socrates in explicating the concept of harmony or consensus, the striving for which characterizes reflective thinking.[6] Ultimately, conscience can lead to a concern about the world, in particular a concern about the extent of harmony in the world. The enlarged mentality of conscience, which causes each of us to consider the future integrity and consistency of the self by reflecting on future states of the self, leads to the inclusion of other selves (external to us) in our imaginings. The conscientious reflection, which begins in an egoistic concern, leads one out of selfish egoism, not by internalizing social rules, it seems, but by making one aware of the value of personal as well as communal harmony.[7]

It seems to me that even with this recognition of the value of communal as well as personal harmony, various restrictions need to be placed on conscience if it is to lead people to pursue the common good. This is so because if one recognizes a particular personal or communal value or good, conscience may motivate one to pursue that value or good relentlessly in order to avoid the negative assessment of the self by the self, which it fears most of all. Indeed, the self might come to form its projects in such a way that the pursuit of a particular role, or good, will dominate all other moral reflection, including that more amorphous reflection that concerns the common good.

A truly enlarged or reasonable conscience is one that takes account of the plurality of roles or goods in a community and seeks to minimize the blind devotion to only one of these that is often said to characterize conscientious behavior. In Sartre's example, the son who believes that conscientiousness requires that he place the immediate needs of his parent ahead of all other goals will become utterly preoccupied with the single-minded goal of serving his parent's needs and preferences. It is more common to find this single-minded attitude in the "private" sphere, although there are some notable cases in the "public" sphere in which there is a single-minded devotion to serving the interests of a particular person or group, for example, among bodyguards or Secret Service agents.

If Sartre's pupil applies conscientiousness to both public and private responsibilities, his dilemma will worsen. He will be reinforced in both his desire to be a dutiful child and his desire to be a dutiful citizen. Sartre recognizes this:

> At the same time, he was hesitating between two kinds of morality; on the one side the morality of sympathy, of personal devotion, and, on the other side, a morality of wider scope but of more debatable validity. . . . But which is the harder road? To whom does one owe the more brotherly love, the patriot or the mother?[8]

For Sartre there are no formulas that will resolve this conflict. But this does not mean that we are left without any guidance. Sartre, like Hannah Arendt, holds to a notion of enlarged mentality founded on the equality of each person as deserving of dignity.

Each person should decide how to act based on a recognition that each of us needs others as much as others need us. We facilitate and thereby share in each other's agency (what some have called "shared subjectivity"), and this should lead us to adjudicate conflicts of responsibility in such a way as to minimize the degradation of others. We should decide as if these others were participating in our decisions. In the end we must act on our own; but our actions should respect the dignity of others. This is the rule of thumb that Sartre and other existentialists believe to be useful in adjudicating conflicts of responsibility.

When individuals recognize that they often share agency or subjectivity with the members of their group, when they recognize that their individual actions have repercussions on the lives of these others of both a direct and indirect sort, then they should also come to a recognition of the connectedness of their lives with other lives in their group. The interdependency that exists in communities, once recognized, makes the members less self-centered and more interested in the interests of others. In interconnected, interdependent groups, one of the prime responsibilities is to maintain the harmony of the group. And one of the chief ways this is accomplished is through the display of respect for each member of the group. Acting in a way which degrades other members disrupts the harmony of the community, in the same way that disregarding an interest of one's own disrupts the harmony of the self. Indeed, given the strong connections between individual and group agency or subjectivity, harming others may literally harm the self.

Pursuing a strategy of reasonable conscientiousness should make it easier, rather than harder, to accommodate conflicting role expectations. Social existentialism stresses that conscientiousness should not involve steadfast adherence to a single value, good, or interest, but that it should involve steadfast striving for accommodation of values within an outlook that is deeply respectful (but not uncritical) of the plurality of values, goods, and interests. To begin such an enterprise, individual conscience cannot be allowed to remain fixated on its own internal harmony, to the exclusion of a consideration of communal harmony. But it is also true that no one should abandon respect for internal harmony. Conflicts can be resolved, when resolution is possible at all, only when people seek an accommodation between their various social roles, seeking first, as we will see, to downgrade those role expectations that deny legitimacy to the interests and values of others in the community, especially those who have traditionally not been afforded dignity.

Communal harmony is best sustained when all of the members of a community are striving to advance the common good. Many of the most serious harms perpetrated within a group are the result of internal conflicts in which one faction is pitted against another. Racism is most intractable in communities in which individual subgroups see their own well-being as at odds with the well-being of another, racially different subgroup. For example, it is common for some lower-middle-class groups of whites to feel themselves so alienated from poverty-stricken Blacks as to think that it is none of the whites' business, indeed perhaps contrary to their interests, to help Blacks get out of dire poverty. If these groups recognize the value of internal harmony, if they grasp the way in which they are interdependent, such factionalized conflicts can be diminished. When the members of a community see themselves as sharing responsibility for the harms that are perpetrated within, and by, their communities, they will come to share a sense of respect for one another that will diminish harm and advance the common good.

3. *Shared Agency and the Problem of Difference*

The proposal I have sketched relies on the idea that each person in a community shares a set of common goods and should strive as much for respect for others and communal harmony as for his or her own self-respect and internal harmony. This thesis is linked to the thesis, defended in various chapters of this book, that people should conceive of themselves as sharing agency with each other. Iris Young, following the postmodernist Julia Kristeva, has argued against communitarian theorists, especially those of the radical left, for espousing an ideal of commonality and unity which "denies difference."[9] Specifically, Young argues that the concept of shared subjectivity, which has been espoused by theorists such as Sartre and more recently Roberto Unger, undermines the legitimacy of different racial, ethnic, and sexual differences, ultimately leading to an anti-liberationist position.

Since my own notion of shared agency has in common with shared subjectivity a number of important features, I will attempt to blunt some of Young's criticisms. In so doing, I will attempt to show why postmodern challenges to shared responsibility should not be accepted. In the final section of this chapter, I will also distance myself from some communitarians who do not espouse limitations on a community's social roles. Nonetheless, it is important that people feel a sense of shared responsibility for what their communities do; feeling motivated to challenge social roles is quite in keeping with shared responsibility. Before turning to the communitarians, I will here consider a few key postmodernist criticisms of the notion of shared agency and subjectivity.

Postmodernists have centered their attention on the attempt in Western philosophy to unify concepts and subjects in ways that deny legitimate differences between them. Iris Young contends that many theorists, including communitarians, participate in what Derrida has called "a metaphysics of presence," which consists "in a desire to think things together in a unity, to formulate a representation of a whole, a totality. It seeks the unity of the thinking subject with the object thought."[10] Jean-Francois Lyotard contends that "the grand narrative" of Western philosophy "has lost its credibility, regardless of what mode of unification it uses, regardless of whether it is a speculative narrative or a narrative of emancipation."[11]

In political philosophy the postmodern challenge often focuses on pseudo-unities that are proposed as facts, but that in reality set up oppositions that arbitrarily separate those who are included and those who are excluded from a shared conceptualization or practice. According to this view, whenever philosophers try to speak of unified or shared conceptual frameworks or practices, they force relevant differences among objects or people to be covered over. Worse yet, an emphasis on sharing leads to a denial of the legitimacy of racial, sexual, or class differences among people. People are irreducibly different; and attempts to emphasize what they have in common run the risk of becoming illiberal or even authoritarian attempts to subjugate those who are different from the majority.

Underlying such a critique is a view of the human person as itself "never a unity, but always a process."[12] As agents we are influenced by a plurality of factors, often from quite disparate sources, that make each of us uniquely who we are. There is a sense of shared identity, insofar as each of us is formed from a common stock of characteristics. But, so the postmodernist would argue, if we reduce these divergent strands to a single unified and shared identity, we deny that which makes each person uniquely who he or she is. In the postmodern view, humans are best understood not as unities but as processes of influences.

Lyotard suggests that if we follow existentialists and other modern thinkers in speaking of the splitting of the self, at least we will achieve "the finality of destroying [the self's] presumptuousness." Doing so would be important, for it would lead to a rejection of any special priority for inner voices or conscience in determining one's obligations.[13] Instead, postmodernists think that humans are best understood, not as self-contained centers of morality, but as intersections of influence. Once again, the self should be seen as a process, rather than as any kind of fixed authority, by appeal to which one can resolve political or moral disputes.

But it seems to me that even if we conceive of the self as a process of influences, we can legitimately see people as sharing agency with one another, insofar as they influence one another constantly to shift their identities based on ever-changing influences from others and the environment. A temporary unity may be created out of these shifting sands; but like a sand castle, it will surely change again and again. In my view, a social existentialist notion of the self (developed in chapter 1), which undergirds shared agency, is not a static conception of the person; the person is not connected in the same way for all time with fellow community members. But an existentialist conception of the self, subject or agent, also stresses that one's social milieu contributes greatly to who one is. The social dimension of the self allows for the characterization of identity as at least partially shared.

To what extent does the social existentialist notion of shared identity or shared subjectivity deny difference? If one believes that what is most important about each person is what that person has in common with others, rather than what somehow makes the person irreducibly different from others, then one has downgraded difference. In ethnic and race relations, the model of assimilation could be cited as epitomizing the denial of difference. Here, what is valued is anything that emphasizes how alike all people are, even to the extreme of advocating interracial and interfaith marriage as a way of further clouding whatever customary or genetic bases there may be for differentiating people.

Postmodernists rightly worry about the loss of ethnic and racial diversity that assimilationist projects would call for.[14] But are there good reasons to think that my view of shared identity and agency is to be so criticized? The notion of shared agency that social existentialism would endorse does not necessarily fall prey to the objection against assimilation. The view I have articulated is a pluralistic view, not one that envisions sharing as a method for rendering all persons the same. To say that all people with racist attitudes share responsibility for racial violence in their communities, as I have argued, is not to say that all differences among these people are to be disregarded. Other characteristics are only temporarily overlooked for the specific purpose of arguing that the shared racist attitudes are an important factor in increasing the likelihood of racially motivated harm.

As a member of a group, a person continues to have an identity of his or her own, although it is a mistake to think of this identity as involving utterly unique characteristics. Indeed, even the radical defender of the social conception of the self can say that it is the multiple and overlapping group memberships that create diversity. There is a sense in which the notion of "being uniquely different" is illusory. If being different is a function of having certain characteristics, and if characteristics are mostly socially generated, then it is unlikely that someone will have a characteristic not shared by at least some other members of a given community, by virtue of which he or she is unique. Being different will be a function of having a unique *combination* of characteristics, each of which is shared by at least some other people. Hence, sharing identity or agency need not deny the uniqueness of whole, complex persons, although it will deny that people have uniquely different characteristics. The claim that social roles are important to moral responsibility need not be interpreted as denying the differences existing among all the people who share these roles. Role responsibility increases or heightens the responsibilities people already have based on their social positions in a community. But given that each person is in many communities and given that each community has a plurality of often overlapping roles, there need be no denial of difference. What does happen is that one is forced to recognize that there are important relationships that make it impossible to understand fully a person's moral responsibilities if that person is conceived of as an isolated individual.

Yet at its most extreme formulation, in the "individualistic anarchism" of Julia Kristeva, postmodernism has found itself reduced to a nonliberationist position concerning moral and social responsibility.[15] If any reference to commonality is necessarily a denial of difference, then the affirmation of difference will only occur when people are viewed as utterly isolated, anonymous individuals, each constituting a unique, differentiated center of morality that excludes consideration of any other persons. This is the position of those individualists I cited as targets of this book in my introductory remarks; they come to urge that we retreat from any form of shared, collective, or social responsibility.

But surely this radical postmodernist view goes too far in reacting to a legitimate worry about some communitarian and social philosophies. Shared agency need not deny difference as long as it retains a pluralistic dimension, as I suggested that it should in the previous section of this chapter. Indeed, the radical individualist position denies commonality to such an extent that it makes the origins of our differences nearly incomprehensible. As an example, Iris Young has with good intentions proposed that we celebrate difference, but that we recognize that minority differences (ethnic and racial, in particular) are both nonreducible to, and ultimately incomprehensible by, those in the majority.[16] But if racial and ethnic differences are incomprehensible, how can those of us in the majority celebrate them? And why think that people from the same type of school system and from the same larger culture are really so completely different in the first place? To do so will, it seems, undermine any legitimate attempts at coalition building (as occurred in Jesse Jackson's Rainbow Coalition). To respect difference, one need not deny commonality;

indeed, to deny commonality is to set the stage for the kind of parochialism and fear of those who are different that is responsible for racial and ethnic bigotry.

My proposal concerning shared agency is pluralistic and respectful of difference but recoils from the radical postmodernist turn toward selfish individualism epitomized by the writings of Julia Kristeva. I turn now to another serious challenge to my proposals, one that comes from those communitarians who see social roles as so important in a person's life as to be nearly beyond challenge. This view goes to the other extreme from postmodernism and denies plurality and radical critique of social roles, even when those roles lead to the abridgment of opportunity and respect for underprivileged racial, ethnic, or gender groups within a community.

4. Communitarianism and Discriminatory Traditions

For many contemporary theorists, there are serious problems with certain versions of liberalism. In my view, the most pernicious problem is that collective action is stymied and individuals are not encouraged to think of responsibility as shared with other members of their community. Communitarians have been at the forefront of those who have criticized liberalism on this score. As should be evident by now, I have drawn on many insights of the communitarian tradition in the construction of my notion of shared agency. But I will now indicate where I part company with some communitarians, especially concerning their lack of sensitivity toward longstanding traditions that have perpetrated ethnic, racial, and gender discrimination.

By stressing the importance of interest groups, pluralistic liberalism is sometimes seen as answering the communitarian challenge to individualism and yet not falling prey to some of the communitarian pitfalls concerning subgroup discrimination. But in U.S. presidential campaigns during the 1980s, special interest groups were vilified from the standpoint of pluralism precisely because they tried to bring considerations of economic and social interests of particular groups into electoral politics. Much of the pluralist tradition, which includes what is called "conservatism" today, has held fast to the liberal denial of the legitimacy of the concepts of shared agency and collective responsibility. Since people are not motivated to think about social problems as requiring joint effort, they tend instead to think individualistically and hence to worry more about possible rights violations from collective social policy than about resolving large-scale social problems.

Certain versions of pluralistic liberalism, epitomized by the views in Will Kymlicka's *Liberalism, Community and Culture*, seek to reverse this trend.[17] They urge us to give greater credence to the importance of protecting groups, especially minority groups, in our concept of rights. Indeed, Kymlicka argues that liberalism does not conflict with the ideal of community, as long as people are conceptualized as tied to one another by

> bonds of mutual respect. And the result of this conception of individual self-direction is not to distance people from each other, but to enable various groups of people freely to pursue and advance their shared communal and cultural ends, without penalizing or marginalizing those groups who have different and perhaps conflicting goals.[18]

I am largely sympathetic to Kymlicka's project. But I think that he and others like him do not realize the extent to which agency and responsibility need to be reconceptualized. Communitarians have also attempted such a reconceptualization, but generally with very conservative and anti-liberationist implications.

I argued in the previous section that insofar as each of us influences fellow community members, there is a sense in which what each of us does is influenced by who the fellow members are. Perhaps more importantly, what a person does is a function, at least in part, of the behavior and attitudes of the rest of the members of the community. We are all implicated in most of the actions taken by our fellow community members. And we all should feel responsible for what occurs or fails to occur within those communities. This is a common theme among many communitarians.[19] For this reason, my social existentialist view may be seen as a variation of communitarianism. But my view also shares certain features with the liberal tradition.

Alisdair MacIntyre and certain Hegelians go quite far in stressing the shared fate of the members of communities. In his influential book *After Virtue*, MacIntyre says:

> For I am never able to seek the good or exercise the virtues *qua* individual. . . . it is not just that different individuals live in different social circumstances; it is also that we each approach our own circumstances as bearers of a

particular social identity. I am someone's son or daughter, someone else's cousin or uncle; I am a citizen of this or that city, a member of this or that guild or profession; I belong to this clan, that tribe, this nation. Hence what is good for me has to be the good for one who inhabits these roles.

But MacIntyre presents us with a nearly static conception of moral responsibility based on social roles. He continues the passage quoted above:

I inherit from the past of my family, my city, my tribe, my nation, a variety of debts, inheritances, rightful expectations and obligations. These constitute the given of my life, my moral starting point.[20]

Like MacIntyre, most communitarians put such a strong emphasis on the connection between one's social roles and one's responsibilities that they neglect the importance of the moral responsibility to reform or to work for the elimination of social roles and traditions that have pernicious consequences, especially for minorities. There are some traditions and social roles, such as apartheid, that should be resisted completely and that should not form the basis for any legitimate duties or responsibilities that people could feel compelled to act upon. Liberalism has been much more clearly opposed to such discriminatory roles and traditions than has communitarianism.

What is worth preserving in liberalism is the strong condemnation of discrimination against minorities. But this idea needs to be mingled with the notion of shared fate and agency, which has been much stressed in communitarian literature. This is not as difficult as it may at first appear, for there is quite a natural fit between the concepts of shared agency and anti-discrimination. Protection of minority rights can often best be achieved when everyone in a community sees that he or she is influenced by and able to influence most other members. In this way, each member of a community sees the problems of minorities as his or her own problems and is motivated to do what is necessary to alleviate the discrimination.

My own "liberationist communitarianism," if in fact this is a good label for it, does not fall prey to the problems that liberal theorists have sketched against more conservative communitarians. The rights of individuals are not submerged in the common good. A concern for shared agency and responsibility is not oppressive of the interests and rights of individuals or subgroups within a community, because a respect for these rights and interests is almost always necessary for communal harmony and hence is a part of the common good. As I suggested above, communal harmony necessitates minimizing degradation and maximizing respect for the members of a community. The abridgment of rights, in most cases, constitutes just this rupture of community harmony. Of course, recognizing their shared responsibilities should have the effect of causing people to be less self-centered and somewhat less concerned about their own interests than they would be if they understood their responsibilities individualistically. But it does not follow from this that others in the society should have a correspondingly diminished interest in the rights of the members of community.

It is beyond the scope of this book to develop a theory of rights from a community or social-group perspective. I have provided the beginning of such a theory in *The Morality of Groups*.[21] We should depart from the view that individual rights are sacrosanct and look at the values that underlie a claim of individual rights. In some cases these very values are better served by the abridgment of individual rights. But in most cases the protection of individual rights is consistent with the goal of communal harmony. The exceptional case occurs when the fulfillment of an individual's claim would disadvantage the members of a group that is already greatly disadvantaged. Of course, in most of these cases, what we are confronted with is a conflict of rights: the rights of the individual versus the rights of the members of the oppressed group, taken individually or collectively. And in such cases, even from a perspective that regards rights as sacrosanct, it is not clear that the rights of the single individual should take precedence over the rights of the group of disadvantaged individuals. In cases in which the individual's rights conflict merely with the interests of the majority, especially if the majority members are relatively well-off compared to the individual, my emphasis on communal harmony would favor the rights of the individual. Communal harmony is not a concept that stands opposed to individual rights. Rather, what communal harmony opposes is the self-centered approach to social problems sometimes mistakenly thought to undergird individual rights. A proper concern for individual rights is based in a concern for distributive justice. There is no *prima facie* incompatibility between concern for distributive justice and communal harmony.

In *On Shared Fate*, Norman Care presents what he calls "shared

fate individualism." He contends that, in light of the large-scale social problems we have been discussing, a person should place service to the interests of others over self-realization in terms of career
choice. Care bases this claim, which is made quite tentatively
throughout his book, on the premise that "all human beings are
equal members of the human community" and that currently some
members of the human community are so destitute that they cannot
achieve self-realization.[22] Care claims that individual responsibility
means being responsible for others as well as for self and that a morally decent form of individualism must recognize that, at least in certain circumstances, people are not entitled to put considerations of
self-realization ahead of service to the needs of others.

While I share many of Care's concerns, I think his own analysis
reveals that individualism and liberalism are at best only partial
foundations upon which to defend shared responsibility. While it is
true that liberal individualism has almost always made room for a
consideration of the interests of others, those interests are normally
only thought to override so-called self-interests when a person's
self-realization is immediately threatened. Homelessness and starvation fit this model well, but the patterns of behavior and attitude
that gradually harm minority group members are not well suited to
the liberal-individualist insistence that something fairly dramatic be
required before an individual thinks that his or her interests should
take a back seat to the interests of others.

My approach is different from Care's approach, in that I have consistently focused on the actual choices that individuals take that, in a
sense, make or could have made a difference in the world. There is
no presumption that self-interest is primary and needs a strong
counterargument to be overridden. Instead, when one's choice concerning attitudes, omissions, or roles, as well as more straightforward direct action, influences the fates of others, then responsibility
kicks in. And for this reason, shared responsibility does not only
concern those extreme situations in which others will be killed or
permanently harmed. Care's shared fate individualism, in the end,
is far too reluctant to address the kinds of "non-emergency" harms
that result from a pattern of practices that adversely affect others. In
this sense, shared fate individualism has some of the same problems
that exist with most conservative communitarian views.

The concept of existential conscientiousness that I sketched at the
beginning of this chapter can address the problems of the more
subtle kinds of harm that result from discriminatory practices and

traditions, largely left untouched by most communitarian and liberal perspectives. Such a view urges us to take the kind of enlarged mentality that is barely individualistic, if at all, for it urges us to look at our roles from the perspective of others who are affected by the way we act within those roles. This means that people need to have an increased sensitivity to all cases in which changes in attitude, action, or inaction have made or could have made a difference in alleviating harm.

Throughout the last three chapters I have begun to explore the limitations on some of the responsibilities people are said to have as a result of their roles. In chapter 7 I explained that philosophers have increased responsibilities due to the roles they have voluntarily undertaken. But I also pointed out that there are some limits to these responsibilities. If it is unreasonable to expect a philosopher to have been able to predict certain harms resulting from his or her philosophizing, then it is a mistake to say that he or she is responsible for those harms, even though they resulted from the philosopher's pursuit of his or her roles. Foreseeability and reasonableness are limits on most of a person's role responsibilities.

In chapter 8 I argued that people in certain communities share responsibility for harms perpetrated by those communities by virtue of having assumed membership in those communities. But I pointed out that there are ways of distancing oneself from the community sufficiently to relieve oneself of such responsibilities. Throughout chapters 7 and 8, I have argued that attempting to stop one's fellow community members from engaging in harm, or at least condemning their harmful behavior, limits the responsibility a person otherwise has by virtue of being a member of a particular group.

In the present chapter I have indicated that if the pursuit of a particular role is necessary to avoid harm to one person, but if that role itself contributes to the subordination or subjugation of a minority within a community, then one may not be responsible for the harm that results from failing to fulfill that role. In Sartre's example, while it may be true that failing to serve conscientiously in the role of son will have harmful consequences on the mother, the son may not be responsible for these harms if the role itself contributes to serious social harms or if it conflicts with other, more socially beneficial social roles. The moral status of a role, the lack of fulfillment of which causes harm to some one person, has limitations based on a wider, enlarged consideration of the social dimensions of one's situation.

Also in this final chapter I have indicated that a concern for communal harmony does not mean that individual rights will be disregarded. The liberationist emphasis of my account continues to be strongly influenced by a concern especially for the individual rights of those who are already disadvantaged in the society. This emphasis, normally identified with the liberal tradition, remains important to my account and is the chief reason why I part company with so many contemporary communitarians. In most cases, a concern for communal harmony should lead to protecting rather than abridging the rights of individuals, although those same individuals should be less self-centered in the way they understand their responsibilities.

The concept of shared responsibility, which is the cornerstone of my "liberationist communitarianism," is more demanding than the conception of responsibility in most versions of liberal individualism, just as it is more liberationist than most other versions of communitarianism. The chief liberationist dimension of my account involves the proposed change in the range of harms for which people hold themselves responsible. When people regard harms that have largely been perpetrated by others as in some sense their own responsibility, they will be more strongly motivated than before to attempt to prevent those harms from continuing or recurring. But there is an important sense in which my account leaves this up to the individual person, for I have not here presented a new basis for holding people subject to punishment. My perspective is different from the liberal perspective, in that it sets the standard of responsibility much higher than the minimalist liberal standard of restricting responsibility only to harms a person directly causes. But there has also been a weakening of what is thought to follow from the judgment that someone is responsible for a given harm. What often follows, in my view, is that a person should be ashamed of or tainted by his or her association with the harm and should try to make amends in the future. But punishment or even feelings of moral guilt are often not appropriate here. This means that, as is almost always true in morality, the liberationist dimension of my account is ultimately up to the individual person rather than primarily a matter for social sanction.

In a revealing interview, Helmut Kohl, former chancellor of West Germany, spoke about German responsibility for Nazi aggression on the fiftieth anniversary of the opening of World War II. He said, "We should beware of making hasty judgments from today's vantage point. Who among us can say with a good conscience that, confronted with such an evil, he would have summoned the strength to be a martyr?"[23] Shared responsibility does not mean that people should feel motivated to become martyrs in order to attempt to stop their fellow community members from perpetrating harm. But it does mean that often people should submit to the enlarged mentality of their consciences the question of whether they have done enough to distance themselves from a harm being perpetrated in their communities.

At the beginning of this book I quoted Hannah Arendt as saying that our membership in a community creates a price that we must all pay.[24] We are now in a position to understand the basis of her claim. As members of communities (whether they be professional associations, universities, or larger social groups), we derive various benefits, which change the scope of our responsibilities. The shared responsibility we should feel for the harms perpetrated within our communities is precisely the cost we incur by being members of those communities. But because we rarely think about responsibility in communal terms, it is difficult for most of us to accept these responsibilities. My book will have succeeded if it has made it more plausible to think of moral responsibilities as shared, and not just individual.

—

Notes

Introduction

1. Mary Midgley, "The Flight From Blame," *Philosophy* 62 (1987): pp. 271–91.

2. See Bernard Williams, *Moral Luck* (Cambridge: Cambridge University Press, 1981); Stuart Hampshire, "Public and Private Morality," in *Morality and Conflict* (Cambridge: Harvard University Press, 1983); and Susan Wolf, "Moral Saints," *Journal of Philosophy* 79, no. 8 (August 1982): pp. 419–39.

3. See Karl Jaspers, *The Question of German Guilt* (1947), trans. E. B. Ashton (New York: Capricorn Books, 1961).

4. See Immanuel Kant's discussion of the attitude of beneficence in *Grounding for the Metaphysics of Morals* (1785), trans. James W. Ellington (Indianapolis: Hackett Publishing Company, 1981), p. 11.

5. See Michael Stocker, "The Schizophrenia of Modern Moral Theories," *Journal of Philosophy* 73, no. 14 (August 12, 1976): 453–66.

6. Annette Baier, *Postures of the Mind* (Minneapolis: University of Minnesota Press, 1985), p. 70.

7. Hannah Arendt, *Eichmann in Jerusalem* (New York: Viking Press, 1963).

8. See Gregory Mellema, *Individuals, Groups and Shared Moral Responsibility* (New York: Peter Lang, 1988), pp. 57–60.

9. Larry May, *The Morality of Groups* (Notre Dame: University of Notre Dame Press, 1987).

1. Existentialism, Self, and Voluntariness

1. Joel Feinberg, *Doing and Deserving* (Princeton: Princeton University Press, 1970), p. 196.

2. See John Martin Fischer, "Responsiveness and Moral Responsibility," in *Responsibility, Character and the Emotions*, ed. Ferdinand Schoeman (Cambridge: Cambridge University Press, 1987).

3. Harry Frankfurt, "Alternate Possibilities and Moral Responsibility," in *Moral Responsibility*, ed. John Martin Fischer (Ithaca: Cornell University Press, 1986), pp. 145–46.

4. Albert Camus, *The Myth of Sisyphus*, (1942), trans. Justin O'Brien (New York: Vintage Books, 1955), pp. 88–89.

5. Ibid., pp. 90, 91.

6. Ibid., pp. 5–6.

7. Jean-Paul Sartre, *Being and Nothingness*, (1943), trans. Hazel Barnes (New York: Washington Square Press, 1966), p. 707.

8. Ibid., p. 708.

9. Jaspers, *The Question of German Guilt*, p. 32.

10. Ibid., p. 71.

11. Sartre, *Being and Nothingness*, p. 710.

12. Jaspers, *The Question of German Guilt*, p. 74.

13. Sartre, *Being and Nothingness*, p. 13.

14. Ibid., p. 87.

15. Ibid., p. 711.

16. Jaspers, *The Question of German Guilt*, p. 36.

17. Martha Nussbaum, *The Fragility of Goodness* (Cambridge: Cambridge University Press, 1986), p. 5.

18. See A. A. Long and D. N. Sedley, *The Hellenistic Philosophers* (Cambridge: Cambridge University Press, 1987), pp. 357–59. I am grateful to Hud Hudson for directing me toward this text.

19. Thomas Hobbes, *Leviathan*, ed. C. B. Macpherson (Penguin Books, 1968), p. 207.

20. John Locke, *Second Treatise of Government*, ed. C. B. Macpherson (Indianapolis: Hackett Publishing Company, 1980), Section 179, p. 93.

21. See Richard Bernstein's article on Dewey in *The Encyclopedia of Philosophy*, ed. Paul Edwards (New York: Macmillan, 1967), especially pp. 384–85.

22. Michael Sandel, *Liberalism and the Limits of Justice* (Cambridge: Cambridge University Press, 1982), p. 183.

23. Charles Taylor, *Sources of the Self* (Cambridge: Harvard University Press, 1989), p. 15.

24. Ibid., p. 26.

25. For a representative sample of some of these thinkers, see Peter Singer's anthology *Applied Ethics* (Oxford: Oxford University Press), 1986.

26. Of the many discussions of these topics, two come immediately to mind: Susan Moller Okin, *Justice, Gender and the Family* (New York: Basic Books, 1989); and Bernard R. Boxill, *Blacks and Social Justice* (Totowa N.J.: Rowman and Allanheld, 1984).

27. Robert Merrihew Adams, "Involuntary Sins," *Philosophical Review* 94 (January 1985).

28. Ibid., p. 3.

29. Ibid., p. 5.

30. Ibid., p. 13.

31. See Ibid., pp. 14–17.

32. Ibid., p. 8.

33. Ibid., p. 17.

34. Ibid., p. 27.

35. Ibid., pp. 26–27.

Notes to Pages 32–41

36. Ibid., p. 17.

37. See Susan Wolf's essay "Moral Saints."

38. See John Arthur, "Rights and the Duty to Bring Aid," in *World Hunger and Moral Obligation*, ed. William Aiken and Hugh LaFollette (Englewood Cliffs N.J.: Prentice Hall), 1977.

39. See the collection of essays entitled *The Virtues: Contemporary Essays on Moral Character*, ed. Robert B. Kruschwitz and Robert C. Roberts (Belmont, Cal.: Wadsworth Publishing Company, 1987).

2. Shared Responsibility and Racist Attitudes

1. President Beering's statement was issued as a memorandum to the entire Purdue faculty.

2. A number of authors have called for expanding our conception of responsibility to include attitudes and character traits. See Charles Taylor, "Responsibility for Self," in *The Identities of Persons*, ed. Amelie Oksenberg Rorty (Berkeley and Los Angeles: University of California Press, 1976), pp. 281–99; and Jon Elster, *Ulysses and the Sirens* (Cambridge: Cambridge University Press, 1979), part 2. Also see the excellent collection of essays, *Responsibility, Character and the Emotions*, ed. Ferdinand Schoeman.

3. I have written on the subject of collective responsibility in some detail, most recently in chapter 4 of *The Morality of Groups*. By the end of this chapter, I will address the question: Can a member of a group be personally responsible for sharing attitudes with those other members of the group who cause harm as a result of having these attitudes? In cases of this sort I am not interested in the *collective* responsibility of the group itself, but only with the *personal* responsibility of the individual member of a group for his or her attitudes that risk harm.

4. I here follow an analysis of the normal relationship between agency and responsibility which H. L. A. Hart and A. M. Honore develop in great detail in the first sections of their book *Causation in the Law* (Oxford: Clarendon Press, 1959).

5. W. Paige Keeton, ed., *Prosser and Keeton on the Law of Torts*, 5th ed. (St. Paul: West Publishing Company, 1984), pp. 322–23.

6. Ibid., p. 323 (note 7).

7. Ibid.

8. Ibid., p. 346. *Prosser and Keeton* offers a justification similar to that offered for certain types of collective action: "In legal contemplation, there is a joint enterprise, and a mutual agency, so that the act of one is the act of all, and liability for all that is done is visited on each." But *Prosser and Keeton* here fails to distinguish concerted action from collective action. The cases that fall under the category of joint tortfeasor are cases of concerted action and should not be handled in the same way that cases of collective or corporate action are handled. Joint tortfeasor cases differ from cases of collective action in that in the former it is not necessary that there be some kind of collec-

tive decision. Furthermore, the type of responsibility that is in question in joint tortfeasor cases is distributional rather than nondistributional. Joint tortfeasor cases are more properly cases of shared responsibility than collective responsibility. It is my view that each tortfeasor should be only partially responsible for the tort because each has merely shared in the tort's production.

9. Bernard Williams has argued that luck does matter in the moral assessment of people's behavior and character. See his *Moral Luck*, especially pp. 20–39. Williams is mainly concerned about the kind of case in which luck leads to good consequences that the agent could not have known would occur. In such cases, Williams argues that our moral assessment will be affected by whether these good consequences result or not. But in the cases I am examining, people are not taking risks out of a hope that greatly beneficial consequences for self or others will occur. Rather, they are taking risks hoping, if hoping at all, merely that greatly harmful consequences to others will not occur. Whether or not Williams's position is plausible (I do not find it so), the difference in our cases should lead to different intuitive judgments. In my cases people are taking risks with the lives of others, and without the consent of these others. On this point, Judith Jarvis Thomson provides a basis for seeing the intuitive difference. See her essay "Imposing Risks," in her book *Rights, Restitution and Risk*, ed. William Parent (Cambridge: Harvard University Press, 1986).

10. Judith Jarvis Thomson provides an interesting analysis of the relationship between this case and other examples of risks in "Imposing Risks," especially pp. 181–83.

11. See Sindell v. Abbott Laboratories, 26 Cal. 3d 588, 163 Cal. Rptr. 132, 607 P. 2d 924 (1980). The *Chicago Tribune* reported that in DES cases the theory of "market-share liability had been adopted in one form or another by the supreme courts of four states—California, Washington, Wisconsin, and New York. But the Illinois Supreme Court rejected the idea in a 5–2 decision." See *Chicago Tribune*, July 4, 1990, sec. 1, p. 7.

12. This was one of many excellent objections raised by Patricia Greenspan, my commentator at the APA Eastern Division meetings, December 1988, where I read a shortened version of this chapter. The point has also been pushed with great vigor by Roger Gardner, to whom I am indebted for lengthy discussions of possible rejoinders.

13. Herbert Morris, *On Guilt and Innocence* (Berkeley and Los Angeles: University of California Press, 1976), p. 135.

14. For a contrasting view, see Joel Feinberg's treatment of the case of collective guilt of all Southern white racists in his essay "Collective Responsibility," in *Doing and Deserving*, pp. 247–48. Also see Howard McGary's reply to Feinberg in "Morality and Collective Liability," *Journal of Value Inquiry* 20 (1986): pp. 157–65. Both of these essays are reprinted in the anthology *Collective Responsibility*, ed. Larry May and Stacey Hoffman (Savage: Rowman and Littlefield, 1991).

3. Insensitivity and Moral Responsibility

1. Iris Murdoch, *The Sovereignty of Good* (London: Routledge and Kegan Paul, 1970; Ark, 1985), pp. 34, 37, 52. A number of recent authors have also advocated a return to an appreciation of the role that perceptiveness or attentiveness plays in morality. See Martha Nussbaum, "'Finely Aware and Richly Responsible': Moral Attention and the Moral Task of Literature," *Journal of Philosophy* 82, no. 10 (October 1985). Also see Sara Ruddick, "Maternal Thinking," *Feminist Studies* 6, no. 2 (Summer 1980); and Lawrence A. Blum, *Friendship, Altruism and Morality* (London: Routledge and Kegan Paul, 1980), pp. 129–39.

2. There has been quite a lot of discussion on the concept of care in feminist moral theory. See Carol Gilligan's *In a Different Voice* (Cambridge: Harvard University Press, 1982). For a representative sample of more recent work see *Women and Moral Theory,* ed. Eva Feder Kittay and Diana Meyers (Totowa N.J.: Rowman and Littlefield, 1987).

3. See Larry Blum's "Compassion," a very helpful discussion of the role of identification in compassion, in *The Virtues: Contemporary Essays on Moral Character,* ed. Kruschwitz and Roberts, pp. 229–36.

4. There are many good discussions of moral-sense theory. See James Bonar, *Moral Sense* (New York: Macmillan, 1930); D. D. Raphael, *The Moral Sense* (London: Methuen, 1947); W. H. Hudson, *Ethical Intuitionism* (London: Macmillan, 1967), chapter 4; J. L. Mackie, *Hume's Moral Theory* (London: Routledge and Kegan Paul, 1980), pp. 12–34.

5. See Gary Watson, "Virtues in Excess," *Philosophical Studies* 46 (1984). Watson argues that a virtue should be defined as: "a characteristic readiness to feel, desire, deliberate, choose, and act well in certain respects. So construed, virtues cannot be excessive and cannot themselves lead to bad action" (pp. 58–59).

6. Aristotle, *Nicomachean Ethics,* trans. W. D. Ross, Book 3, chapter 5.

7. See Holly Smith, "Culpable Ignorance," *Philosophical Review* (1983): p. 570.

8. See William Lyons's very thorough discussion of the various bases for blaming a person for his or her emotions in his *Emotions* (Cambridge: Cambridge University Press, 1980), chapter 13.

9. *Webster's New Twentieth Century Dictionary,* 2d ed. (1978). For a philosophical analysis of this concept, see Marilyn Friedman and Larry May, "What's Wrong with Stereotypes?" *Proceedings of the Ohio Philosophical Association Annual Meeting* (April 20, 1985): pp. 88–100.

10. Murdoch, *The Sovereignty of Good,* pp. 66, 38.

11. Harry Frankfurt, "Freedom of the Will and the Concept of a Person," in *Moral Responsibility,* ed. Fischer, pp. 65–80. Also see Frankfurt's essay, "Alternate Possibilities and Moral Responsibility," in *Moral Responsibility,* pp. 143–52.

12. Ibid., p. 80.

13. See Marilyn Friedman's very insightful criticisms of Frankfurt in her essay "Autonomy and the Split-Level Self," *Southern Journal of Philosophy* 24, no. 1 (Summer 1986): pp. 19–35; and Irving Thalberg, "Hierarchical Analyses of Unfree Action," *Canadian Journal of Philosophy* 8, no. 2 (June 1978).

14. see John Elster, *Ulysses and the Syrens* (Cambridge: Cambridge University Press, 1979), p. 105; and Charles Taylor, "Responsibility for Self," in *The Identities of Persons*, ed. Rorty, pp. 281–300. For a very different kind of argument, see Robert Merrihew Adams, "Involuntary Sins."

15. See Gordon Allport's seminal study *The Nature of Prejudice* (Garden City, N.Y.: Anchor Books, 1958).

16. Jean-Paul Sartre, *The Emotions: Outline of a Theory*, trans. Bernard Frechtman (New York: Citadel Press, 1948), p. 45.

17. Sartre, *Being and Nothingness*, p. 726.

18. Sartre, *The Emotions*, p. 45.

4. Groups and Personal Value Transformation

1. For a discussion of some of the ontological underpinnings of this analysis, see chapter 1 of my *The Morality of Groups*.

2. Steven Lukes has a very interesting discussion of the varieties of viewpoint that are often labeled "individualist." See his *Individualism* (Oxford: Basil Blackwell, 1973).

3. An important exception to the individualist bias in medical ethics literature is the special volume of *The Journal of Medicine and Philosophy* on collective responsibility in medicine, ed. Edmund Pellegrino and Lisa Newton, 7, no. 1 (1982).

4. Of the many studies that have been done, Gustav LeBon's *The Crowd: A Study of the Popular Mind* (London: T. Fisher Unwin, Ltd., 1896), is still one of the most often cited.

5. See, for example, Rom Harre's *Social Being* (Totawa N.J.: Littlefield, Adams and Co., 1980).

6. See *The Morality of Groups*, especially chapters 1 and 2.

7. See John C. Hughes and Larry May, "Sexual Harassment," *Social Theory and Practice* 6, no. 3 (Fall 1980).

8. See Benjamin Freedman's "Health Professions, Codes, and the Right to Refuse HIV-Infected Patients," *Hastings Center Reports* (April–May 1988): pp. 22–24.

9. See Thomas Hill, Jr., "Servility and Self-Respect," in *Rights*, ed. David Lyons (Belmont Cal.: Wadsworth Publishing Company, 1979).

10. David J. Hickson, Richard J. Butler, David Cray, Geoffrey R. Mallory, and David Wilson, "Comparing 150 Decision Processes," in *Organizational Strategy and Change*, ed. Johannes M. Pennings et al. (San Francisco: Jossey-Bass Publishers, 1985), p. 140.

11. See Jonathan Bennett's excellent essay, "The Conscience of Huckelberry Finn," *Philosophy* 49 (April 1974): pp. 123–34.

12. Harper Lee, *To Kill a Mockingbird* (1960; New York: Warner Books, 1982), pp. 156–57.

13. On role differentiation in organized groups, see Cecil A. Gibb, "Leadership," *The Handbook of Social Psychology*, 2d ed., vol. 4 (Reading, Mass.: Addison-Wesley Publishing Company, 1969).

14. See my paper "On Conscience," *American Philosophical Quarterly* 20, no. 1 (January 1983): pp. 57–67.

15. Susan Budassi Sheehy and Janet Barber, *Emergency Nursing: Principles and Practices*, 2d ed. (St. Louis: C. V. Mosby Company, 1985), pp. 16–17.

16. See Jane Sharkey's essay "Learning not to Understand," *Nursing Times*, April 17, 1985, p. 50. Also see my essay "Insensitivity and Moral Responsibility," *The Journal of Value Inquiry* 26 (1992): 7–22.

17. See Peter French's introductory chapter in his anthology *Individual and Collective Responsibility: The Massacre at My Lai* (Cambridge, Mass.: Schenkman Publishing Co., 1972).

18. Richard Zaner, *Ethics and the Clinical Encounter* (Englewood Cliffs N.J.: Prentice Hall, 1988), p. 318.

19. See Herbert Morris's essay "Shared Guilt," in *On Guilt and Innocence*.

20. For more of the details of this argument see my *The Morality of Groups*, chapter 4.

5. Negligence and Professional Responsibility

1. Keeton, *Prosser and Keeton on the Law of Torts*, pp. 163–64.

2. Ibid., pp. 164–65.

3. See Virginia Held's essay "Can a Random Collection of Individuals Be Morally Responsible?" *Journal of Philosophy* 68, no. 14 (1970): p. 479.

4. Robert Merrihew Adams, "Involuntary Sins," p. 19.

5. Aristotle, *Nicomachean Ethics*, Book 5, chapter 8, 6–7 (1136a5–10).

6. Herbert Fingarette, *On Responsibility* (New York: Basic Books, 1967), p. 42.

7. See Ronald Milo's *Immorality* (Princeton: Princeton University Press, 1984), pp. 102–3.

8. Bernard Williams, "A Critique of Utilitarianism," in J. J. C. Smart and Bernard Williams, *Utilitarianism: For and Against* (Cambridge: Cambridge University Press, 1973), p. 116. Williams develops the notion of negative responsibility as part of a critique of utilitarianism and is not directly interested in the notion of negligence. Yet many of his examples are easily applicable to negligence.

9. *Black's Law Dictionary*, 5th ed. (St. Paul: West Publishing Co., 1979), p. 931, gives a definition of "criminal negligence" similar to that of Prosser and Keeton for negligence in tort law: "Criminal negligence which will render killing a person manslaughter is the omission on the part of the person

to do some act which an ordinarily careful and prudent man would do under like circumstances, or the doing of some act which an ordinary careful, prudent man under like circumstances would not do by reason of which another person is endangered in life or bodily safety; the word 'ordinary' being synonymous with 'reasonable' in this connection."

10. A. D. Woozley, "Negligence and Ignorance," *Philosophy* 53, (1978): p. 293.

11. Christine Sistare, *Responsibility and Criminal Liability* (Dordrecht: Kluwer Publishing Company, 1989), p. 137.

12. H. L. A. Hart reached a similar conclusion in his famous essay "Negligence, *Mens Rea* and Criminal Responsibility," (Oxford: Oxford University Press, 1968), pp. 151–52. He asserts that "*if* anyone is *ever* responsible for *anything*, there is no good reason why men should not be responsible for such omissions to think, or to consider the situation and its dangers before acting."

13. *Black's Law Dictionary*, pp. 1089–90.

14. See my essay "Professional Action and the Liabilities of Professional Associations," *Business and Professional Ethics Journal* 2, no. 1 (Fall 1982): pp. 1–14, for more details of this analysis of the moral status of professions.

15. See Hannah Arendt, *Eichmann in Jerusalem*.

16. Bernard Williams takes a similar line in his hypothetical example of "Jim," who is told that he can save the lives of nineteen South American Indians by shooting a twentieth Indian himself. Since the Indians' trouble is not due to any positive acts of Jim, it would violate Jim's moral integrity, Williams claims, for him to act contrary to his conscience and shoot one of the Indians. See Williams, "A Critique of Utilitarianism," pp. 98–99.

17. If Eichmann had felt that exterminating Gypsies and Jews was the right thing to do, his life might have been easier to integrate; but other aspects of morality would then be implicated. I follow Hannah Arendt in thinking that people rarely, if ever, set out voluntarily to do harm to fellow human beings. Most great evil is perpetrated negligently, rather than intentionally. See Arendt's essay, "Thinking and Moral Considerations," *Social Research* 38, no. 3 (Autumn 1971).

6. Collective Inaction and Responsibility

1. See chapter 4, sections 1 and 2, of my *The Morality of Groups*, for a discussion of collective responsibility of organized groups.

2. I am thinking of cases in which a harm occurs today as a result of actions taken by a corporation many years ago. In such a case, the corporation is responsible, and yet no current members of the corporation are responsible.

3. In action theory the distinction between refraining and inaction for individuals is often drawn in terms of whether there is any action not performed. Myles Brand and others contend that the person who is asleep is

said to be *inactive*, since sleeping does not involve actions that are not performed, whereas the person who chooses not to go to the movies *refrains* from performing an action, namely, going to the movies. I will use these terms somewhat differently with respect to groups, but I think that the distinction between a group deciding not to act, or collectively omitting to act, and merely not acting, or engaging in collective inaction, would not be opposed by those who proposed the distinction. See Myles Brand, "The Language of Not Doing," *American Philosophical Quarterly* 8, no. 1 (January 1971): pp. 45–53.

4. David Copp argues that even less cohesion than results from solidarity or commonality of interest may suffice for collective predication. In chapter 10 of his forthcoming *Morality, Skepticism and Society,* Copp contends that "consensus over options for the group" is sufficient, when the members "share an interest that will be served by" a collective action, "but they each may not take an interest in the realization of that interest by the others." I believe that *shared* responsibility may exist when each member of a group shares an interest that would be served by a group's action or inaction. But *collective* responsibility demands a stronger condition than this. "Collective responsibility" is not a mere shorthand expression for the responsibility of the members; rather it is the responsibility of the group as a whole. For it may be that the members of the group remain truly unconnected in their shared interests, such that it would make more sense to talk of "aggregated interests" than "collective interests." The group must be capable of intentional action for collective responsibility to be ascribed; with merely a consensus of unrelated opinions, there is no sense in which the "decision" of the group is intentional.

5. Virginia Held, "Can a Random Collection of Individuals be Morally Responsible?" p. 479.

6. Robert Goodin, *Protecting the Vulnerable* (Chicago: University of Chicago Press, 1985), p. 137.

7. I discuss these issues of group ontology in the first two chapters of *The Morality of Groups.* I have not previously examined groups with so little cohesion as the ones discussed here.

8. See Peter French, *Collective and Corporate Responsibility,* (New York: Columbia University Press, 1984), especially chapter 1. Peter French is correct to distinguish collectivities from aggregates in terms of whether moral judgments are appropriately made of the group itself, as is true for collectivities, or whether the judgments made about the group are merely shorthand for judgments made about each member considered aggregately. French and I part company on the issue of whether collective action and collective responsibility must entail some kind of collective entity or agent. French says that various organized groups should be conceived of as full-fledged moral agents, while I deny this claim.

9. Gregory Mellema has a very interesting discussion and defense of this position, which he calls "moderate anti-dilutionism." See his book *Individ-*

uals, Groups and Shared Moral Responsibility. Also see Michael Zimmerman's essay "Sharing Responsibility," *American Philosophical Quarterly* 22, no. 2 (April 1985): pp. 115–22.

10. John M. Darley and Bibb Latane, "Bystander Intervention in Emergencies: Diffusion of Responsibility," *Journal of Personality and Social Psychology* 8 (1968): pp. 377–83.

11. L. Jonathan Cohen, "Who is Starving Whom?" *Theoria* 47, part 2 (1981): p. 80.

12. See Peter Singer, "Famine, Affluence, and Morality," *Philosophy and Public Affairs* 1, no. 3 (Spring 1972). Singer argues that the number of people who could do something about world hunger should not affect the extent of each person's obligation. Hence he contends that we should not take numbers into account when discussing the moral obligations of the members of a group. As he puts it, "People in the same circumstances have the same obligations" (p. 234). But Singer is willing to recognize that what others have done, or can be expected to do, is part of the consideration of circumstance that may change a person's obligations.

13. See Susan James's essay "The Duty to Relieve Suffering," *Ethics* 93 (October 1982): pp. 4–21.

14. W. H. Walsh, "Pride, Shame and Responsibility," *Philosophical Quarterly* 20, no. 78 (January 1970): pp. 1, 13.

7. Philosophers and Political Responsibility

1. Richard Rorty's speech was delivered on November 1985 in Guadalajara, Mexico. The speech was printed in *The Proceedings and Addresses of the American Philosophical Association* 59, no. 5 (June 1986): pp. 747–53.

2. See the two essays following Rorty's, by Ofelia Schutte and Thomas Auxter, in the *Proceedings* (June 1986): pp. 753–59.

3. In this and subsequent quotations from Plato, I will quote from G. M. A. Grube's translation of *The Trial and Death of Socrates* (Indianapolis: Hackett Publishing Company, 1975), 30e–31a.

4. Ibid., 33b.

5. For more details of this view, see the monograph I coauthored with Martin Curd, *Professional Responsibility for Harmful Actions* (Dubuque: Kendall Hunt Publishing Company, 1984).

6. William Earle, "The Political Responsibilities of Philosophers," *Ethics* 79, no. 1 (October 1968): p. 10. Earle argues that philosophers have neither a greater nor a lesser responsibility in the political realm than average citizens. I address arguments of this sort in section 3.

7. On this point see Richard Wasserstrom's essay "Lawyers as Professionals: Some Moral Issues," *Human Rights* 5, no. 1 (1975): pp. 1–24.

8. Alan Goldman, *The Moral Foundations of Professional Ethics* (Totowa N.J.: Rowman and Littlefield, 1980), p. 1.

9. As just one example, see page 53 of Walter Kaufmann's translation of

Nietzsche's *On the Genealogy of Morals* (New York: Vintage Books, 1969), which has a footnote by Kaufmann that reads: "Having said things that can easily be misconstrued as grist for the German anti-Semites, Nietzsche goes out of his way, as usual, to express his admiration for the Jews and his disdain for the Germans."

10. The best commentary on this distinction is still Hart and Honore, *Causation in the Law,* especially chapter 3.

11. Letter from Nietzsche to Karl Knortz, June 21, 1888, in *Nietzsche: A Self-Portrait from His Letters,* ed. and trans. Peter Fuss and Henry Shapiro (Cambridge: Harvard University Press, 1971), p. 119.

12. Ibid., p. 135. Letter from Nietzsche to Peter Gast, December 8, 1888.

13. See Michael Levin's letter in the *Proceedings of the American Philosophical Association* 63, no. 5 (January 1990): pp. 62–63. There he claims that "Blacks are significantly less intelligent than whites" and uses this claim to buttress his conclusion that philosophers should "regard themselves free of any discriminatory guilt" concerning the small number of Blacks in our profession.

14. See Patrick Riley's discussion of this point in *The General Will Before Rousseau* (Princeton: Princeton University Press, 1986). He claims, on page 7, that as early as the seventeenth century in France "*volonté generale* figured in high politics; it didn't have to wait for Robespierre's transmogrified Rousseaueanism." Also see the collection of essays on this subject in *Jean-Jacques Rousseau: Authoritarian Libertarian?*, ed. Guy H. Dodge (Lexington: D. D. Heath and Company, 1971).

15. John Gardner, *On Moral Fiction* (New York: Basic Books, 1978): pp. 105–6 and elsewhere.

16. The most recent essay on this controversy is Michael Zimmerman's "The Thorn in Heidegger's Side: The Question of National Socialism," *Philosophical Forum* 20, no. 4 (Summer 1989): pp. 326–65.

17. For quite a different but not incompatible argument, that philosophers constitute a community with responsibilities as a group, see Julius Moravscik's "Communal Ties," the presidential address at the Pacific Division meetings of the American Philosophical Association, printed in *Proceedings and Addresses of the American Philosophical Association* 62, no. 1, supp. (September 1988): pp. 221–23.

18. See my essay "Professional Action and the Liabilities of Professional Associations."

19. Jurgen Habermas, "Work and Weltanschauung: The Heidegger Controversy from a German Perspective," *Critical Inquiry* 15, no. 2 (Winter 1989): p. 453.

20. See Robert Strikwerda's essay "On What Ought We Vote? On Professional Organizations and Public Affairs," in *Social Policy and Conflict Resolution,* ed. Thomas Attig et al., Bowling Green State University Applied Philosophy Program (1984). Strikwerda sets up criteria for deciding when it is legitimate for professional organizations to vote on political matters.

21. On this point see Virginia Held's helpful set of arguments for the obligation of philosophers to speak out on political issues, in *Rights and Goods: Justifying Social Action* (New York: The Free Press, 1984), pp. 10–11.

22. On this point see Arnold Davidson's essay "Questions Concerning Heidegger: Opening the Debate," *Critical Inquiry* 15, no. 2 (Winter 1989): pp. 407–26.

8. Metaphysical Guilt and Moral Taint

1. Jaspers, *The Question of German Guilt*, p. 36.

2. Paul Ricoeur, *The Symbolism of Evil*, trans. Emerson Buchanan (New York: Harper and Row, 1967), p. 269.

3. Those interested in pursuing the view that we are all responsible for everything should consult Herbert Morris's attempt to defend this notion in his essay "Shared Guilt." In chapter 1, I labeled my own view "social existentialism" to distinguish it from those early existentialist positions that deny the importance of social groups in the formation of the self and in the understanding of the limits on our moral responsibilities.

4. Jaspers, *The Question of German Guilt*, p. 71.

5. Ibid., p. 74.

6. Jean-Paul Sartre, *Anti-Semite and Jew* (1948), trans. George J. Becker (New York: Schocken Books, 1965), p. 90.

7. Ibid., especially p. 91.

8. Ibid., p. 141.

9. See Thomas R. Flynn, *Sartre and Marxist Existentialism* (Chicago: University of Chicago Press, 1984), p. 8.

10. John-Paul Sartre, *What is Literature?* trans. Bernard Frechtman (London: Methuen, 1950), p. 45. Sartre makes a similar point concerning the moral responsibility of the writer: "If the writer accepts being the creator of injustices, it is within a movement that points beyond them to their abolition."

11. See Allport's classic, *The Nature of Prejudice*.

12. Jaspers, *The Question of German Guilt*, p. 36.

13. Anthony Appiah, "Racism and Moral Pollution," *Philosophical Forum* 18, nos. 2–3 (Winter–Spring 1987): pp. 185–202. Appiah is hesitant to draw this conclusion (on p. 201) and, to be fair to him, his conclusion is quite qualified. But at the end of his essay he does announce that a belief in taint is not a good reason to cease to be a consequentialist.

14. Ibid., pp. 186, 187.

15. Arthur Adkins, *Merit and Responsibility: A Study in Greek Values* (Oxford: Oxford University Press, 1960), p. 86.

16. Ibid.

17. Ibid., p. 99.

18. Appiah, "Racism and Moral Pollution," p. 190.

19. Ibid., p. 191.

20. Thomas Jefferson's letter to Samuel Kercheval, July 12, 1816, in *Thomas Jefferson on Democracy*, ed. Saul K. Padover (New York: Mentor Books, 1939), p. 63.

21. See Sartre, *Being and Nothingness*, p. 710.

9. Role Conflicts, Community, and Shared Agency

1. Jean-Paul Sartre, "Existentialism is a Humanism," in *Existentialism from Dostoevsky to Sartre*, ed. Walter Kaufmann (Cleveland: Meridian Books, 1956), pp. 295–96.

2. Hart, *Punishment and Responsibility*, p. 213.

3. Sartre, "Existentialism is a Humanism," p. 297.

4. Philippa Foot, "Virtues and Vices," in *Virtues and Vices and other Essays in Moral Philosophy* (Berkeley and Los Angeles: University of California Press, 1978), p. 8.

5. Arendt, "Thinking and Moral Considerations."

6. Ibid., p. 439. I here rely on Hannah Arendt's interpretation of the *Apology* and *Gorgias*.

7. For a more detailed analysis see my paper "On Conscience."

8. Sartre, "Existentialism is a Humanism," p. 296.

9. Iris Young, "The Ideal of Community and the Politics of Difference," *Social Theory and Practice* 12, no. 1 (Spring 1986): p. 1.

10. Ibid., p. 2.

11. Jean-Francois Lyotard, *The Postmodern Condition*, trans. Geof Bennington and Brian Massumi (Minneapolis: University of Minnesota Press, 1984), p. 37. Also see Anthony Cascardi's article "Narration and Totality," *Philosophical Forum* 21, no. 3 (Spring 1990).

12. Young, "The Ideal of Community and the Politics of Difference," cites Julia Kristeva on this point, p. 4.

13. Jean-Francois Lyotard, *The Differend*, trans. Georges Van Den Abbeele (Minneapolis: University of Minnesota Press, 1988), p. 107.

14. Young, "The Ideal of Community and the Politics of Difference," p. 13.

15. "Individual anarchism" is used by Terry Eagleton and Toris Moi to describe Kristeva's political philosophy. For an excellent account and critique of the underpinnings of this view, see Dorothy Leland's essay "Lacanian Psychoanalysis and French Feminism: Toward an Adequate Political Psychology," *Hypatia* 3, no. 3 (Winter 1989).

16. Young, "The Ideal of Community and the Politics of Difference," pp. 19–21.

17. Will Kymlicka, *Liberalism, Community and Culture* (Oxford: Clarendon Press, 1989).

18. Ibid., p. 254.

19. For instance, early medieval communitarians stressed the interdependence of members of a monastic community and their shared responsi-

bility for one another. See the Rule of St. Benedict, chapter 23, where it is said that the monks "are to have not even their bodies or their wills in their own keeping." The prime directive was to be "Let all things be common to all."

20. Alisdair MacIntyre, *After Virtue* (Notre Dame: University of Notre Dame Press, 1981), pp. 204–5.

21. See my *The Morality of Groups*, especially chapters 5–7.

22. Norman Care, *On Sharing Fate* (Philadelphia: Temple University Press, 1987), pp. 29, 192.

23. Quoted in the *Chicago Tribune*, September 13, 1989, section 1, p. 1.

24. See Hannah Arendt, "Collective Responsibility," (1968), in *Amor Mundi*, ed. J. W. Bernauer (Dordrecht: Martinus Nijhoff Publishers, 1987), p. 50.

Index